Other books by Addison Gayle, Jr.

THE BLACK AESTHETIC

BLACK SITUATION

BLACK EXPRESSION

BONDAGE, FREEDOM AND BEYOND: *The Prose of Black Americans*

OAK AND IVY

CLAUDE MCKAY: *The Black Poet at War*

THE WAY OF THE NEW WORLD: *The Black Novel in America*

WAYWARD CHILD
A Personal Odyssey

ADDISON GAYLE, JR.

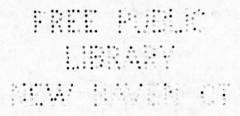
ANCHOR PRESS/DOUBLEDAY

GARDEN CITY, NEW YORK

1977

Library of Congress Cataloging in Publication Data

Gayle, Addison, 1932–
Wayward child.

1. Gayle, Addison, 1932–
2. Critics—United States—Biography.   I. Title.
    PS29.G3   813'.5'4 [B]
        ISBN 0-385-08873-6
Library of Congress Catalog Card Number 76-42329

For Adell

CONTENTS

I went to the rock to hide my face, the rock cried out, "No hiding place, no hiding place down here."

Anonymous

This is the urgency: "Live! and have your blooming in the noise of the whirlwind."

Gwendolyn Brooks

CHAPTER 1

To look back into the past of one's life is difficult. This is so, primarily, because experiences of the past appear at present sometimes like a giant collage, one set of experiences blending, meshing into another. When I sat down to begin delving into my own past, therefore, I was aware that in order to give form and structure to the experiences of my life, to shape and reorder the past, that I would have to rely upon my own remembrances, some few minor documents, now dimly recollected impressions, and that I would never know how much more important the things remembered were than the things forgotten. When finally I began to write the first draft of my autobiography and as I completed one grueling page after another, after days of staring at blank sheets of paper, more days of beginning and tearing up scribbled notes, I discovered that the memories seemed not so much like a collage, but like many varied dreams connected, somehow, one to another . . .

From this perspective in time, the incidents which occurred in 1938, when I was only six years old, appear fantasized, dreamlike . . .

I remember standing outside the John Marshall elementary school in Newport News, Virginia, on a bright, beautiful May day, one among many other students. Blue sky and white fluffy clouds reigned overhead, freshly trimmed green grass, beneath my feet. The boys and girls were dressed in blue and white—the girls in white dresses, blue sashes, and black patent leather shoes, the boys in blue jackets, white pants, and navy blue neckties. For this May Day celebration, the teachers had designated Alexander, the son of the town's only Black banker, as grand marshall. A mulatto, he was resplendent in long white pants and covering blue jacket; and the pants and jacket were set off by an expensive blue tie, matching the sash about his waist. I recall looking in his direction, making faces, trying to attract his attention, because two days before during lunch period, he had noticed me, spoken to me.

I had been elated. The most popular student in school, a mulatto, had singled me out. I had begun to fantasize, imagined that we were related or, at best, close friends. I wanted him to notice me during the May Day celebration, acknowledge our friendship before the others. Instead, he began barking out commands, and, obeying, we fell in line—boys in one, girls in the other. Mildred, who was also mulatto—her mother was a teacher—had been designated grand marshall for the girls. The two marshalls moved down parallel lines, inspecting our attire. Eyes closed, body trembling slightly, I listened to Alexander, commenting as he moved from one boy to the other: "Nice outfit, fellow; you standin tall, man. Smart tie, there." As he approached me, I opened my eyes, apprehensively, thought back to the day in the lunch room. He walked around me, once, twice, shook his head, boomed loudly: "Short pants or bloomers?"

Someone snickered.

He continued: "You call that a jacket? Is this a tie or a rag?"

Abruptly, the snickering ceased! My embarrassment, I suppose, became the embarrassment of them all. They wanted to claim part of my shame, I think, to feel something of my sorrow. This was worse than their snickering and I hated them for it. I bowed my head, searched the grass, was almost oblivious to Alexander's parting remark: "We want lots of improvement next year . . . in everything . . ."

He moved down the line. I wanted to call him back, to tell him —but I was ashamed—that next year I would probably wear the same outfit, that short pants were cheaper than long pants, that to make a necktie out of an old throwaway dress was cheaper than buying one, that my father was no longer with us, that my mother worked two jobs in order to feed my sister and me.

But I did not want to bore him with my tales of poverty. I

knew that he had never sat awake, reading at night, and been thrown into terror by the gnashing sound of rats attempting to cut through nailed-up tin covers, that he had never heard their whining and crying as they streaked along the walls, never felt the gnashing of their teeth against the coverings, as though they were needle pricks upon the nerves. He had never awakened in a cold sweat, after dreaming that the rats had broken free and were coming, millions of them, charging upon the little army cot situated between the stove and the kitchen cabinet, coming, cold, wet, furry, like an army of the enraged, the demonic. I could not tell him these things, because I wanted him to like me.

I accepted the rightness of his criticism, just as I accepted the rightness of the criticism of others, those like Doretha, for example. Doretha, who sat behind me in class, was fat, overweight, but she had light skin and long hair—two long dark brown plaits. Though I was fond of her, she ignored me, whispered to her friends and mine that I was Black and ugly. Perhaps, I thought, she was right; and perhaps, too, this is why I admired Alexander. He was neither Black, ugly, nor poor. And perhaps this is also why I envied him—envied him his curly hair and light skin, envied him his home without rats.

I did not know then why, conversely, I was afraid of people like Alexander and Doretha, or why I wanted to protect myself from them, and believed that I could do so by becoming like them, that if I had light skin and curly hair, that people would forget my ugliness, would not threaten me, would not shame me.

That night, on the army cot in the kitchen, as I lay listening to the rats, I felt the day's embarrassment, felt my ugliness. Only the noise that came from the front room, where Clarissa and her boyfriend were, interrupted my thoughts. Clarissa, daughter of a friend of my mother's, sometimes baby-sat for us. On such nights, usually, she would have an argument with her boyfriend, who came to keep her company. I heard the old argument, again, on that night, heard her say to her boyfriend, "I cain't do nothin like that in Miss Carrie's house, she might come home." Shortly after, I heard the door slam violently, and heard Clarissa come into the kitchen, move over to my cot. She sat down beside me, and I turned, facing her; she pulled off my undershirt, then my shorts. She moved into bed with me, pulled her dress up around her waist, stroked me between the legs, placed my hands between her legs. As she maneuvered me on top of her, put me into her, and began moving underneath me, I thought, "Clarissa likes me better than her boyfriend."

I thought that I liked her too, but always, I thought of Doretha, wished that Clarissa was Doretha, that she was light-skinned like Doretha, that she was not Black and ugly like me.

I did not go to sleep when Clarissa left, but lay face up to the ceiling, listening to the rats. I knew when the door leading from the kitchen to the bedroom was closed, and I knew also that this meant that the madonna had come home with a man. Above the noise of the rats, I listened to them making love, and though I did not know the man, I hated him, wished that I were a god so that I could destroy him. I did not want him doing to her what Clarissa had done to me. I put a pillow over my head, not wanting to hear the noises, wishing that I could run away. I did not realize it then, but the first flowering of rage had begun, manifested itself as never before, in my desire to escape, to run away, to sleep so long and so soundly that, when I awoke, the events of yesterday would have faded from memory.

At the age of six, then I began plowing under my past, trying to bury unpleasant experiences, and in so doing, was unable to understand many of the changes occurring within me as I moved through ages seven to twelve. Others noticed the changes, undoubtedly, but either paid little attention to either them or to me, or were not sophisticated enough to interpret certain nuances of character as rebellious or deviant. One person who recognized the changes was Mrs. Logan, who had been my first-grade teacher. I remembered her in that first year of school as a kind woman, who smiled a great deal, who treated me fondly. When she became my homeroom teacher, as I advanced to the seventh grade, the changes discernible in our relationship, I attributed to her and not to myself. She scolded me often, kept me late after school, would sit glowering at me from behind small eyeglasses. She would tell me she did not know me anymore, that I was not the little boy she had known in the first grade. This remark would be followed by a litany of my criminal acts, none of which I considered criminal at the time. I picked on the other children, she avowed, talked back to adults, called students such derogatory names as black dogs, and dirty stinking niggers.

I would listen to her tirade, roll my eyes up toward the ceiling, tell myself silently that her animosity had nothing to do with the crimes she enumerated, that she, like the others, students and teachers, was jealous of me because I read real books instead of *Dick and Jane*. I recall—always with pride—the day she told me to shut up when I had interrupted the class by loudly telling a friend about a story by Dostoevski. I recall how, afterward, she had kept me after school and told me that I was not better than the other students just because I could read and write well and score high on tests.

But I believed that I was better, much better. None of the others—not even the mulattoes (but I never thought I was better than they were!)—had read Dostoevski, none of them knew anything about Raskolnikov, none of them could imagine themselves being, as I could, Raskolnikov. And the others, even the mulattoes, listened to me and noticed me when I told them the story of *Crime and Punishment*, told them of murder and violence, drew pictures of Raskolnikov as a bold man, afraid of nothing, defiant of everything. How much of the story I really understood, I do not know. The book fascinated me, however, and I embellished it anew with each telling. No matter the true nature of Dostoevski's character, I portrayed him as a great fighter, the hero of the poor, a man of intense violence. I acted out his supposed disdain and haughty air, in and out of the classroom, exhibiting his arrogance, boasting of violence and action in what I imagined to be his manner whenever Ollie, Horace, and I met to go car hunting.

Ollie and Horace, my closest friends, were neighbors and during the summer months—when we were allowed to remain out of doors after dark—we would go over to Madison Avenue and Twenty-seventh Street—two blocks away, where the prostitutes gathered to wait for their predominantly white customers.

The white men drove up in their cars, waited for a prostitute to come over, whispered something to her, and, if she got into the car, drove a short distance away—one block to an empty lot. With bricks in our hands and pockets, we would wait until there were a number of cars in the lot, before throwing the bricks, sometimes denting fenders, breaking windshields. One time Ollie hit a man, who was on his stomach, in the back seat having sex with one of the girls. Usually, however, we aimed only for the cars. One night I threw two bricks and both hit a Studebaker.

The man jumped out of the back seat and looked around. We unloaded the rest of our bricks at the man and ran away.

One night, after we had hunted seven cars, and returned to our hangout corner, near Woodward's drugstore, I wondered what the white men had thought, wondered if they had been afraid. I didn't believe that they were, because I did not believe, then, that white people were afraid of Black people. I wondered about the Black men who were sometimes in the cars with the girls, wondered why they did it. This point brought forth an argument between Horace and Ollie and myself. They did not want to throw at the cars with Black men in them and I did. They said that the Black men were the same color as the girls, and that that was all right. The white men, however, they argued, should stay over town in the white section, where they belonged, and not bother the Black girls, because if we went over town and bothered their girls they would lynch us.

Speaking, as I imagined Raskolnikov might, I said boldly, "We ought to lynch the white men! If they can lynch us, then we ought to lynch them."

"You always talking bout hurtin somebody." Ollie replied.

"Like with Merlin." Horace said. "You said you gon kill Merlin, didn't ya?"

I remember clenching my fists, and replying loudly, "I will. If Merlin bothers me, I'm going to kill him." I walked away, sat on Mr. Rooks' car, which I cleaned every Sunday morning. Merlin was the neighborhood bully and since reading *Crime and Punishment*, I had often wondered what it would be like to kill him. I thought also of Clarence, who lived next door to my aunt on Hampton Avenue. One day he fought a boy from Newsome Park, on Jefferson Avenue, near the five-and-dime store. Clarence kicked the other boy in his privates and the boy, grabbing his crotch, backed all the way into the five-and-dime store glass window. I imagined that I would like to have been Clarence, imagined that I did something like that to Merlin.

Horace moved to sit beside me on the car. He said, "If you fight Merlin, you got to fight him fair."

"If I fight Merlin," I replied, "I'll hit him with a bottle."

Horace said, "If you fight somebody and they fight you fair and you don't fight them fair, then you a coward."

I did not want to be a coward, but I could fantasize hitting

Merlin with a bottle, watching the blood gush from his head, even though, then as now, whenever I saw blood or thought very long about it, I began to feel strange, could not imagine myself as Raskolnikov any longer, was sickened by the idea of violence. To see someone bleed is to be propelled back to the time when I had watched my father bleeding thick red blood, which gushed as from a fire hydrant from the wound in his head. I remember that he and the madonna were fighting, again, that he had her down on the floor, was choking her, and that though I was frightened, I leapt upon his back, trying to pull him away. He struck me with the back of his hand, stood up from the madonna, came to kneel over me as I sat rubbing the side of my face. I remember the perspiration on his forehead, the red in his eyes, the pointing finger, the harsh, shouting voice.

"You leave that child alone!" I remember the madonna shrieking out, remember that he ignored her, said to me, "You *my* boy, hear me. You don't take up for that bitch."

I remember too that I stood up slowly, crawled over into a corner, wanted him to stop shouting at me, wanted him to take me in his arms—something he did no longer. I was crying loudly, covering my face with my hands; so I did not see the madonna swing the bottle. And I looked up again only when he yelled out, saw him reel, sway, saw the blood come pouring from his head, saw the madonna with the bottle in her hand, heard her screaming, "You leave my child alone!" I remember that I never saw her swing the bottle, that I continued to sit in the corner, watching the blood spurt from my father's head.

This was before we moved away from my father, before I was old enough to know about books, before I began to read Dostoevski, before Mrs. Logan discovered that I had changed, before I had decided that I was going to be a famous writer. My father not only gave me books by Russian writers, but also by Black writers. Among these, Richard Wright was my favorite. I had read only a few of the stories in *Uncle Tom's Children*, and had not become fixated, in my fantasy, on any one character, as I had with Raskolnikov. No, instead of imagining myself as one of Richard Wright's characters, I imagined myself as Richard Wright. I imagined people looking up to me as a famous writer, asking for my autograph, seeking me out. I imagined that I was rich and famous, and that I was as good as people like Alexander, and that I bought a big house for my mother and sister, and that I had Mr. Walter killed for hurting my mother.

I knew that he hurt her often. She did not realize that I knew, does not, perhaps, even to this day, know that I knew. One day while playing in the backyard, I looked into the window of our kitchen and saw him hit her with his fists. She fell on the floor, started crying, pleading. Another time, she came home late one night, told me to get up and go sleep in her room. She held her coat bunched up against her side but I could still see the blood. Mr. Ernest, a neighbor, came to help. I heard her tell Mr. Ernest that Mr. Walter had stabbed her. "You ought to call the cops on that guy," Mr. Ernest said.

"Ernest," she had cried. "I swear fore God, I'm scared. That's one evil crazy nigger, who'd just as soon kill you as look at you and them old police ain't gon do nothin but make him kill me faster."

The next morning I washed the blood out of the sink on the back porch. I hated Mr. Walter and wished that I could kill him. Every day when he came home from work, Momma made me take him his dinner. I wished that I could find some roach poison to put into it. I longed to see him die like a roach, to see the blood squashed out of him and his legs and arms torn off and his eyes poked into with a hot piece of steel. I wanted to see his thing cut out and slit into little pieces and stuffed down his ugly black mouth. I wanted to claw and scrape away all of his skin and pour lye over his flesh and I wanted to tie him to four horses, his legs to two and his arms to the other two and watch as they tore him apart. I would kill Mr. Walter, I promised myself, when I became a man and a famous writer.

These were strange and new thoughts to me, but I did not know that they signaled a change in my character. On that day, therefore, when I was twelve years old and Mrs. Logan had kept me after school, had implored me to tell her what was wrong with me, why I was not like I was when I was a little boy, I had not known what to answer. The truth was that I did not know what was wrong with me. I didn't know what I did at twelve that I hadn't done as a little boy. I remember not paying much attention to her questions, repetitive, anxious, almost pleading questions, because it was a Friday—in two days I would go to visit my father. Ever since my mother took my sister and me away, I had visited my father on Sundays. Each week, usually on Fridays, my palms would begin to sweat, my chest to ache, my pulse to thunder in my temples. These feelings continued until I confronted him on Sunday, and to quell the anxiety, I tried to fill up every hour of Friday and Saturday. I had remained insolent, unresponsive to Mrs. Logan, therefore, not only because I had no answer to her questions, but because I was thinking about playing football for the rest of the evening, and going to the movies with Horace and Ollie on Saturday.

By Saturday morning, when my mother, as usual, gave me the usual fifteen cents to go to the movie, the tension became more pronounced. I held out one of my hands and watched it tremble. I began to imagine what I would say to my father, how I would articulate my words, what gestures I would use. When Ollie and Horace called me out on the back porch, I hesitated, wanting to be alone with my panic. Dismissing them with the excuse that I had to visit my grandmother and aunts, I promised to meet them at two o'clock in front of Woodward's drugstore. The tension abated somewhat as I entered my grandmother's house, seven blocks from my own.

My grandmother was a short, spry Black woman, who liked to hold me and pull me close. Entering the house, I said hello, moved quickly to the icebox to take out a piece of chicken, and went to sit next to her on the couch.

"How your momma?" She asked, running a hand over my head.

"She all right." I said.

"When you seen that no-good daddy of yourn?"

"I saw him Sunday." I replied, my palms heating up again.

She said something else about my mother and father, and I simply nodded my head. I discarded the chicken bones in a plate on the table beside the couch and laid my head on her stomach. She tickled my stomach, laughed, said, "You little devil, what you inchin up to me for now?"

I turned to escape her hands. "Nothin," I said hesitantly. Then, as if in afterthought, "Momma, you got a dime so I can go to the show?"

She laughed, tapped me on the head. "I know you come by here for something. Go look in the bedroom and bring my pocketbook." She gave me a dime.

I went to the icebox, took another piece of chicken, soon returning to her side. She said, "When your momma go to work at the army base, you and Loretta gon eat here when you come from school." She continued: "That crazy daddy of yourn supposed to come by here and see me last week and he ain't got here yet."

She noticed my fidgeting, pulled me close in a bear hug: "All right Mr. Ants-in-the-pants, you go head to the show." I kissed her and walked two blocks away to Aunt Dana's house.

Dana, my grandmother's sister, is my favorite aunt. She is a big, tall brown-skinned woman who wears horn-rimmed glasses.

Whenever I visit her, now, I remember the day when she took me shopping with her, to Martin's department store, over town, where the white people lived. As she looked through lingerie, housecoats, and other women's wear, I stood beside a counter with boys' pants for sale. A white boy, about my age and size, walked to the counter and picked up a pair of pants. Suddenly, a woman appeared, grabbed the boy roughly by the neck, gestured toward me, and began shouting almost uncontrollably. "Don't you see that little nigger next to them clothes? You want to catch something? You want to get sick causa that dirty little nigger?"

Dana dropped whatever she had in her hand, a slip, a dress, something, ran around the side of the counter where the white woman was, slapped her with the back of her hand. Screaming, the woman fell against the counter. Dana hit her again. Two white men came over, one grabbed Dana, the other pulled the woman out of Dana's way. Then a Black man ran over, shouted to the white man, "You take your goddamn hands offa that woman."

More Black people came to surround the two men. The white man released Dana and retreated before the crowd.

"What happened?" the Black man who had come up first asked.

"That white peckerwood," said Dana, "called my nephew a dirty nigger, and I was gonna beat all the white offa her." The white woman was led away. Other white people in the store looked at them—her and her crying little boy—as they walked down the aisle. The crowd of Black people stood waiting for the police, who, after questioning Dana and a few others, ushered the two of us out of the store.

The man who had first run over to help, drove Dana and me back over town. I sat in the back of the car, he and Dana, in front. "These pecks sure scareda somthin these days," the man said. "All these Black soldiers and sailors down here, you know, them boys what come from up North, from New York and Chicago; they don't take no stuff. Them crackers know if they start something them soldiers gone shoot up this mother fu . . ." He glanced at me through the mirror, smiled sheepishly, said, "I means this damn town. They gon burn it to the ground."

"That's right," agreed Aunt Dana, "and they don't lock up no soldiers. They calls the MPs and the SPs. They don't treat colored people like they did before. I'm glad there's a war and all them Black soldiers is here; I wish they would shoot them pecks steada the Japs. I can't stand no peck. The Japanese ought to kill all of em, and if I hada had that little hoer a little longer, I woulda beat all that white stink offa her." She reached into the back of the car, patted my knee. "Ain't that right, Puddin?"

"Unhun," I replied.

"That's his name?" the man asked. "Puddin?"

"Unhun," said Aunt Dana. "He's Addison Gayle's boy."

The man turned around, took a long look at me. "You mean old Gayle, who speaks up there by Brown's poolhall all the time, the one that holds them meetings?"

"That's right," Aunt Dana said, proudly.

"Your daddy is one smart one," the man says. "And he can talk up a storm; lord, that man can talk. And he gives them crackers hell too, you hear me? Yassuh, he tells it just right about them pecks. Um, old Gayle's boy; ain't that something?"

As I walked into the kitchen of Dana's house, without knocking as usual, I remembered that I had never seen the man again. I had always intended to ask Dana about him, to find out whether she had seen him again, but each time I visited her, I was in a hurry to go somewhere else. This time was no exception, and after collecting two pieces of pie, an apple, and twenty cents from her, I kissed her good-by, went to my other aunt's house (Mary), picked up fifteen cents more, a glass of milk, and a candy bar, and reached Woodward's drugstore shortly after two o'clock to find Ollie and Horace all ready there. Together we walked over the bridge to the white people's section of town, to the bakery. We bought day-old doughnuts for a nickle—twelve in a bag—Ollie bought jelly, Horace bought cream, and I bought plain. We bought a big Pepsi-Cola apiece, went to the movies, ate and drank, and watched the pictures three times. Afterward we went home, ate supper, and came back to hang around the drugstore until bedtime.

That night I had difficulty falling asleep. The tension had begun building again. I tried to read, but couldn't concentrate; finally, after my mother shouted for me to turn out the light, I lay on the cot, tossing and twisting my way into Sunday morning.

Sunday morning, I awakened earlier than usual, the tension much more severe. I tried to wash the sleep from my eyes, to still the nervousness in my hands, my stomach, my legs. The tension, the nervousness, as always, I knew would increase, for I could not go to see my father until one o'clock, not, that is, until I had gone to church, paid homage to the God of my mother. I busied myself about the house, lighting the coal stove, washing down the kitchen cabinet, until my mother and the neighborhood awoke. When my mother intruded into the kitchen to begin her Sunday meal of hot rolls, fried chicken and rice, I retired to the corner, tried to read despite my nervousness and the blaring sound of the Dixie Hummingbirds coming from radios up and down the block.

The men had begun to come out of the houses now, shouting across the yards to each other, telling jokes, reminiscing in subdued tones about their Saturday night experiences. Mr. Ernest, our next-door neighbor, issued his weekly call to a comrade: "Hey, Packard . . . old Packard . . . c'mon out here, man . . . git somma this sunshine . . . leave the cookin for the womenfolk . . ."

"Hey, Ernest!" Mr. Packard answered in a loud, booming voice. "How you doin this mornin? What you got for a thirsty man?"

Momma shook her head, laughed, said, "Lord, they startin already."

Mr. Ernest pushed his head through our door. "How yall this mornin?"

"How you, Ernest?" Momma asked by way of replying. "Comon in here and have some breakfast. Be ready in a few minutes."

"Thanks, Carrie, but Martha, she cookin chicken and rice too . . . I'm gon be choppin a minute."

"How Martha? She goin to church today?"

"Yeah, she gon be gitten ready after we eat." He paused, said, "Say Carrie, what was the figure yesterday?"

"It was 609."

"Now, ain't that a doggone shame? I started to play that dang number in combination and some devil made me play 747. You know old Chester what work for Jew Balser? Well, he died the other day, and that's his house number, 747, so I played that stead a 609."

"Well, Ernest, you know you can't tell about them figures. I sticks to my little 724. I play it in combination, but that's all."

"Dang if that ain't the best way, cause you sure can't beat um."

My mother looked in my direction, then to the clock on top of the refrigerator, back to me, said: "Puddin, why ain't you gettin ready to go to church?"

I uncrossed my legs, but made no further movement. I did not want to go to church, was bored by the preaching and singing. Further, I was anxious to get the visit with my father over with, would rather go there, as frightened as I was, than to church.

Momma turned back to Mr. Ernest: "Lord, all that boy wants to do is sit up in the show or somewhere, reading some book; don't want to go to church for nothing in the world."

"That's true, nona these youngons these days care anything about church."

I wanted to ask Mr. Ernest if he was going to church, but I knew that my mother would hit me for sassing an adult. She noticed that I had not moved: "Now, boy, you gon move or do I have to come move you?"

"Momma, Loretta's in the toilet," I shouted defensively, beginning to move in the direction of the bedroom.

"You just found out you got to go to the toilet?"

I removed my blue suit from the nail on the back of the door of the bedroom, heard her shout, "You come back here, boy, and wash up fore you start puttin on any clothes."

As I got the washbasin and started running water, I saw Mr. Ernest shake his head. "One a these days," he says, "they gon be glad we sent um to church."

"Now, ain't that the truth. Course this one here, he like his daddy; he don't believe in no God."

I wanted to shout out that she was right, that I didn't believe in God, because I was a smart boy who reads Dostoevski, and no longer had to believe in fairy tales. I wanted to tell her too that no God would let us be as poor as were were, or let her work as hard as she did. I knew that she would not believe me, would instead blame my father because I did not believe in God. Her talking about my father to Mr. Ernest only increased my anxiety about seeing him later, and renewed my animosity at having to go to church, to go through the ritual. But I could not shut out the sound of her voice emanating, even through the closed bedroom door.

"Ain't no God . . . that's what Gayle always said. Tells me, you make Puddin go to church cause you believe in God, but I don't believe in no God myself." She laughed. "Come tellin me one day: Carrie, you always talkin bout God this and God the other, don't you know God dead? And I just looked at him—Now, Gayle, I said, who don't know that? Everybody know that; they crucified him; he oughta be dead, now, everybody knows that. Well . . . he just stood there, shakin his head."

Mr. Ernest joined her in laughter. "Gon tell you somethin you already know, hunh? . . . Well"—he became serious—"there's one thing bout old Gayle, can't nobody take away . . . He's a smart one alright . . . yassuh, that man is somethin smart."

"Oh, he's smart all right, but that don't get it all the time; you got to be something sides smart in this world."

Fully dressed, I moved back into the kitchen, ignoring my mother's approving glance, and sat down to eat. The Dixie Hummingbirds were singing "Steal Away," and above their voices, neighborhood women could be heard shouting at their children to prepare for church. Momma and Mr. Ernest began talking about the high price of fish and work at the shipyard, but their words no longer registered. In less than two hours, I would see my father. Without waiting for my sister, and without eating all of my food, I started off to church.

My father lived with a woman, Pauline, on Warwick Avenue, about five blocks from where I lived. She was younger than my mother, slim, soft-spoken, and very attentive to my father. She was leaving the house as I arrived, and, greeting her, I realized I would have to confront him alone, and my nervousness increased. I found him standing in the center of a sparsely furnished living room, noticeable for the large stacks of books, thrown carelessly upon makeshift bookcases.

My father was of medium height, with deeply tanned skin, and an almost oval face; his eyes were large, brown, penetrating. I stood watching him, my arms behind my back, my eyes searching the room, wondering if this were the day that he would come over to me, pull me close to him, hold me. Instead, he began, as usual, to interrogate me: "You been a good boy this week? Didn't give your mother any trouble?"

My answers, as always, were mechanical, studied: "No, sir."

"Have you finished that book by Wright yet?"

Embarrassed, I looked down at the floor, said meekly, "I got twenty more pages to go."

His face darkened, he hesitated a moment, reflected, asked, "How is your schoolwork?"

"Fine."

He moved from the center of the floor, speaking as he walked, toward the sofa: "Well, sit down, sit down."

I sat on the sofa, hoping that he would come to sit beside me. He continued walking toward the bookcase, finally paused to lean against it, waited for me to begin a conversation. I did not know what to talk about, was afraid that I might say something wrong, or worse still, something trivial, unimportant. The anxiety was very real for I knew that I was expected to say something, but I did not know what to say, knew that he would stand there, as always, until I had said something, and knew, too, that as soon as I said it, he would counteract it, demonstrate his knowledge and mastery of words.

"You speaking tonight?" I finally blurted out.

"Yes, out in Hampton. I'm running for Congress this year, you know."

"Yes." I knew, but I did not yet know what running for Congress meant.

"Think you're going to win?" I continued, not really caring.

"What kind of a question is that?" he asked accusingly. "Of course I won't win. Those pecks would never let a Black man win."

"Why you running, then?"

"So that one day *you* can win."

His voice was louder and the fact that he spoke directly to me helped to relieve some of the tension, encouraged me.

"Unun," I said, "I don't want to win, I don't want to run for Congress."

He acknowledged my rebuff, slight as it was, with a frown,

arched his eyebrows, interrogated: "And what are you going into, sir?"

I thought for a few moments before blurting out, "I'm going to be a writer like Richard Wright."

His face became impassive, his voice soft, but the put-down was visible, audible: "I hope you learn more about colored people than Wright did."

"He knows a lot about colored people," I ventured, not knowing what else to reply.

"No," he replied, and there was a softness in his eyes now, "he doesn't know very much. The people he knows are all emotional, act on impulse. They never think rationally. A colored man who acts like his people do—like women—can't survive in this white man's world. The white man thinks twenty-four hours a day, and the colored man has to think twenty-eight."

He walked over to sit beside me on the couch, though not very near, and lit a cigarette: "Boy, you think twenty-eight hours a day, you hear me? When you sleeping, you be thinking, you be planning ahead, and you look every step of the way, and know where you are going before you make one move. There's nothing you can do if you don't think; you can't do anything if you're emotional; never let yourself lose control. That's what white people want: colored people who don't think. That's what I always tried to tell your mother, but she wouldn't listen. She always cries and screams and loses control, and listens to them ignorant people down at the church."

He flicked the ash from his cigarette, fixed his eyes upon me, now hard again. "The church teaches colored people not to think. It teaches them to be ignorant and emotional, like the white man wants them to be. You go to church, like your momma tells you on Sunday—you obey your momma—but you sit there and think and analyze everything they tell you; don't believe nothing they tell you—nothing nobody tells you, until you think about it first."

I wanted to reach out and touch him, to ask him to hug me, to allow me to bridge the distance between us. I wanted him to know that I tried to follow his precepts to the letter, that I always thought about everything, tried to do what he wanted me to do, would want to be what he wanted me to be, was frightened that maybe I could not be. "I always think about everything," I said, wanting to move closer to him, wanting to keep talking to him.

But he stood, reached into his pocket, gave me a quarter, said, "That's a good boy."

It was his way of dismissing me and I resented it. But I did not want to incur his disfavor, thought that maybe I shouldn't burden him by wanting to stay with him so long, that I should not always be so afraid, before coming to see him, that he would be angry with me, scold me for saying something stupid, and tell me not to return.

That night, after supper, after washing the dishes, I took the folding cot from behind the door in the bedroom earlier than usual and began reading the last pages of Richard Wright's *Uncle Tom's Children.*

CHAPTER 2

To no one's surprise—least of all his own—my father did not win his race for Congress, though he did, as I was to discover years later, make a respectable showing for a Black candidate in Virginia. If there was any disappointment in his life during those years of the forties, it was not congressional elections or the small number of Blacks he was able to attract to the Communist party. What dismayed him was mainly the irrationality of the war years and the exuberance and false hopes which those years engendered. The American campaign to dehumanize the enemy—the Japanese and Germans—was carried on nowhere with more vigor than among the Black population of Newport News, Virginia.

Crudely distorted pictures of Tojo and Hitler lined the windows of banks, department stores, and the NCO clubs of the area. Children were taught by their parents and teachers that Germans and Japs were subhuman species who were attempting to enslave everyone, especially Black people. Except for a few disgruntled Blacks, none made the skin-color identification between the Japanese and Black people. Pledges of allegiance to the flag and the singing of "America the Beautiful" began every class session, and few days passed when we were not reminded of the heroism, sainthood, and benevolence of Franklin D. Roosevelt.

The benevolence, at least, seemed unquestionable. Only a few years back, I seemed to remember, I would stand in line with my mother, over town, where the white people dispensed sacks of corn meal and slabs of white meat, growing impatient as we were pushed further and further to the back of the line whenever a white person came to receive his depression year's rations.

By the forties, the depression years became diffused in memory. Jobs were plentiful and well paying. My mother worked at one of the army bases and it seemed we had moved from poverty to affluence overnight. There was now money for me to join the Boy Scouts—first, the Cub Scouts, and then at the age of fourteen, the regular units. I made frequent trips to summer camps, where we swam, hunted, fished, and made floats depicting the villains of the war. In addition, I was able now to earn my own money, graduating from a corner shoeshine box to the shoeshine shop on the main street in the Black neighborhood, near the bars and whorehouses, where the soldiers, sailors, pimps, and whores congregated.

The ability to earn money, plus the experiences of growing up destroyed the comradeship between myself and my friends. We seldom met at Woodward's drugstore any more, and playing car hunting seemed a game for younger kids. Moreover, approaching the age of fourteen, I felt that I had outgrown my friends, become so much more sophisticated than they, learned so much more. I continued to read avidly, not only the books my father gave me, but those I was able to buy myself. My grades in junior high school were superior and the envy of the other students, and I was no longer shunned by the mulattoes, by those like Alexander and Doretha.

The war years, it seemed, had meant a converging of old antagonists; white people seemed now more solicitious of Blacks, scarcely ever insulting, even willing to relax some of the segregation rules. I recall with embarrassment, the day I had gone to the post office to mail a special delivery letter for my mother: while daydreaming, I had walked over to get a drink of water and inadvertently began drinking from the fountain labeled "white." Sensing that I was committing a crime, I had stopped in the middle of the flow, splashing water upon my chin, looking sheepishly at the white man who stood beside me, ready to apologize. The man waved my apology aside: "Gon, boy, get yourself a good drink; it all come from the same place." Uncomfortably, I finished my drink, offered my apologies anyway, and walked quickly out of the post office.

Some sort of détente had also occurred between Blacks and

mulattoes. The high-paying jobs at the shipyard had attracted
black lawyers and teachers—who worked there during the summer
months—most of whom comprised the mulatto class, and with
the breakdown of the barriers of poverty, occupation, and status,
had come, somewhat, the breaking down of the barriers of skin
color. Though most of the mulattoes still lived in the two-story
houses near the end of the Black part of town, parents who took
part in bond drives and war chest ceremonies, brought their children along and friendships and liaisons were formed among the
young and the old.

The breaking down of the barriers afforded me an opportunity
to ingratiate myself with the mulattoes. I began to associate with
them at school, ignoring my darker friends, to fantasize romantic
liaisons with girls with light skin and long hair. I paraded my
knowledge of books before them in order to impress—and began
writing poetry—scribbled lines, romantic vignettes, about the
girls. They tolerated me, perhaps found me amusing, sometimes, I
thought, laughed at me secretly. No matter; more and more I
began to copy their movements, their gestures, their way of speaking, their arrogant manners and their seeming disdain for Blacks
of darker skin color.

Their reluctant acceptance of me, due to ingratiation on my
part (I always knew the answers to exam questions, could
straighten out the grammatical flaws in a composition) coupled
with our seeming affluence and the exuberance and the energy of
the war years, made me more independent. I was more prone to
challenge my father's judgment, to respond to his questions more
boldly, less nervous when contemplating a visit to him, which
now was very rare.

The rarity of our meetings was due not to me, but to him. He
was too busy now, holding meetings, speaking in different places.
On those occasions when I did see him, I began to notice him
drinking more heavily. He alone, I believe, realized the illusionary
tenor of those years, sensed the decline to follow the war—that
slipping back to yesteryear, when poverty and antagonisms dominated the Black community. Had I known his feelings then, I
would not have shared them.

For me, these appeared the golden years—not so much, I know
now, because they *were* golden—but because years and events
seemed to move so rapidly. I graduated from junior high school,

scoring the highest grade on a state exam for students, Black and white. With the money I made shining shoes and running errands for the pimps and prostitutes, I began to buy my first clothes, to call on girls for the first time—mulattoes. As I entered my freshman year at high school, I had my first real sexual experience, outside of Clarissa, with a classmate on the grass, in back of our junior high school.

I joined the high school choir, tried out for the football team, joined the high school drama club and played the convict in *Great Expectations*. I began almost nightly to write poems, then short stories, finally trying my hand at a play, and later a novel.

The writings, as I remember them now, however, were more revealing of my true feelings during these years than I could then have discerned. Except for those few secret pieces written to light-skinned girls whom I fancied relations with, the pieces spoke of loneliness and despair, of silent pain and intensive longing. Through tone they told the other story, revealed the pessimisms clouded by futile optimism. For though I would not have admitted it then—I needed to create a world of my own, peaceful, fanciful—the rage and resentment which had marred the earlier years, had not disappeared, but increased. There was silent rage at the madonna, for the succession of men awarded favors I could not receive; at the baby sisters who continued to come; at the high school teachers who began to treat me as a pariah, mainly, I suppose, because there was nothing significant about me except for the fact that I was bright. I used this intelligence unsparingly, as my weapon, at every occasion. Despite the new affluence, the new generations of rats were as bold as ever, and entire walls of the kitchen were now almost barricaded by sheets of tin.

Relations with my father grew more strained as I began to visit mulatto girls, to see *their* fathers lavishing attention upon them. I began to realize, consciously for the first time, what it meant not to have someone to talk to regularly, to ask questions of, to feel close to, to be held by.

The writings did not reveal all of this, but the tone did. It revealed a bitterness and hostility which led me into short periods of depression, hours in which I had to be alone, walking through the parks or along the waters near the beach at the edge of the city. More and more, I was thrown back upon myself, forced to come to grips with feelings which I could not recognize. Though I would often return from these solitary sojourns refreshed, imitating Frank Sinatra singing "Over There," the thunderclouds had begun to roll, were filled to overflowing, destined, one day, to erupt.

The storm clouds had been gathering also over the new optimism brought to the Black community as a result of the war years. They erupted on the day the atomic bomb brought defeat to Japan and an end to the war.

Within one year, my mother had lost her job at the army base, and joined hundreds of unemployed Black men and women, their livelihood denied now that the shipyard had fewer orders to fill. The soldiers and sailors, with their money and their bravado in confronting whites, had gone and the white population resumed their distance and acts of intimidation against the Black population. The mulattoes, forced now out of jobs where their status was equal with that of other Blacks, returned to their less lucrative professions. Once more, they established themselves as a class, distinct and apart. For us, my mother's unemployment brought back, almost immediately, the old poverty, sending us to the welfare rolls. My inability to make money reduced my wardrobe, ended my trips to summer camp, made me morose and more enamored than ever of my mulatto friends. Though maintaining relationships with me, they did so despite the coolness directed toward me by their parents.

Alice, daughter of my former elementary school teacher, her skin as white as any white person's, her hair long and silky, continued her relationship with me, despite the coolness of her parents —and even my mother's disapproval. "You keep runnin behind that old yella gal," my mother admonished me one night as I prepared to visit Alice, "and you know them people don't want you over there."

She was right. Now that old animosities had resumed between the Black and mulatto communities, my presence was tolerated only because I spoke well and had nice manners—characteristics which moved me somewhat out of the "common nigger" class. The Chandlers were no "common niggers," far from it. The father was now principal of an elementary school, and the mother, a party-giving socialite who sometimes gave away old clothes to the people in my neighborhood, few of whom accepted them. Unlike her brother John, Alice was something of a rebel. She talked back to her mother, I had noticed, sassing her most of the time, doing as she liked. During one of my self-doubting moments, which came more rapidly now, I had asked her why she went out with me, hoping for a flattering reply. Alice answered, "Because I want to. You're so reserved and shy," she teased me, "but you're smart, no matter what the teachers say."

I was, indeed, flattered, but I didn't believe her. Having done nothing to ingratiate myself with her as I had with others, I could not understand why she wanted to go out with me, unless, of course, she felt sorry for me. As an extension of her mother and father, Alice was clean and pretty, and I was ugly, poor, and Black. Furthermore, I knew that Herbert came to see her also. He was light-skinned too, with good hair, the son of a doctor, the idol of the other girls at Huntington. No, she did not really like me, only felt sorry for me, or perhaps continued to see me only to infuriate her parents. I did not, however, resent her for this. I felt somehow as if I deserved to be tolerated, to be pitied.

I had been seeing her for two months (having met her during my freshman year at high school, but only getting up the nerve to ask her out one year later) when we both served on the student council together. My difficulties with teachers, more pronounced then, had earned me sympathy among the students—a sympathy reserved for underdogs—and among some members of the faculty the open hostility between us had filtered down through the tightly knit mulatto community of schoolteachers. I was not surprised, therefore, when, upon calling on Alice one evening, I was met at the door by her father, who did not attempt to disguise his hostility. "I hear tell you in trouble at school again."

Not knowing which trouble he was referring to, I politely answered, "No, sir, not me."

"Miss Frazier was by here," he said, ignoring my reply, "and she said they talking about expelling you up there. Say you a smart aleck, a know-it-all."

"That's not true," I said, being sure to pronounce my words distinctly. "Miss Frazier and Miss Smith don't like me; they don't want me to run for vice-president of the student council, because they think I will win. They want Rebecca to run." I did not tell him that Rebecca was light-skinned, or remind him that her mother was a teacher in his school.

He bristled, perhaps because he surmised what I wanted to tell him, by implication. "Boy don't you stand there and call no teacher a liar in front of my face."

I retreated a few steps, averted his eyes, and said by way of apology, "I'm not calling her a liar, but she asked me why I wanted to be vice-president—like I wasn't good enough—and I said, I just did."

He frowned, shook his head, and without offering me a seat called upstairs for Alice. Confused, angry, and nervous, I sat on the edge of a chair, looking away from him, wanting to talk to him, to tell him of the injustices enacted against me, to plead my case, to gain his approval. I wanted to tell him about the oratorical contest in which I had been engaged only three months ago. There had been two other contestants: Barbara, whose mother was a social worker, and William, whose father was a lawyer. The contest was sponsored by the Elks Club, held annually, and local winners went on to regional, and, perhaps, national contests. English teachers—Miss Frazier, Mr. Jones, and Mr. Calloway served as the school judges. Barbara, who spoke first, had talked of the commitment of Black youth to education and pointed out the work needed to uplift the race. She received a loud ovation from students and teachers. Having chosen a second-place ballot, I followed Barbara, and had spoken of the necessity of education and its importance in bringing about change. Education, I argued, made rational thinking possible, and the problems that confronted us as people could be met only by carefully analyzing and thinking about our situation. My gestures—facial, hand waving—the intonation and emphasis of words were patterned after my father, whom I had watched speak on Sunday afternoons down at the poolroom. I inserted quotes from W. E. B. Du Bois and Monroe Trotter into my address. When I finished, the applause was much louder than it had been for Barbara— students and some teachers rose to their feet in a standing ovation. Though William's speech was not bad, the decision, everyone knew, was between Barbara and me.

I knew that I had done very well, believed that I had won, though I knew that the teachers would not admit this and reward me. The wartime camaraderie was ended and the old strictures would be held against me. My father was not a teacher, doctor, or lawyer; he was a Communist, and worse, a poor one. My family was poor and my background consisted of no middle-class ancestry

familiar to the community. Neither was I a model student. I questioned teachers, refused to accept the pronouncements of my
elders/superiors as gospel. I knew things that one of my complexion and family situation should not have known: I knew of Tolstoy
and Dickens, of Claude McKay and James Weldon Johnson, of
Karl Marx and Friedrich Engels. Except by a few teachers—Mrs.
Greene and Mr. Johnson, and Mr. Rainey come quickly to mind
—I was considered a troublemaker and a smart aleck.

I wanted to tell Alice's father, also, what the teachers thought
about boys like me. Those of us whose parents had neither money
nor status were destined to end up in the shipyard. According to
state law, each student was obligated to attend school until the
age of eighteen. The educational objective, for those like me, was
to keep us until we reached the age limit. If we learned something
in the interval, good; if not, it didn't matter. This state of affairs
angered my father, who, in conjunction with the Party, had, at
one time, attempted to replace the shipyard-owned and -managed
union with one managed by the workers. "Them damn people at
Huntington," he said one day, "they against us. They got things
all worked out with the white people. They supply the poor
Blacks to do the dirty work. The white boys—most of them have
no education at all—get jobs as supervisors, ledermen, mechanics
—the Blacks all go to the riggers, the cleanup crew. Ninety-nine
per cent are pure Black; only one per cent mulatto. They are poor
and uneducated and think they're being done a favor to be able to
work, though they are paid less than white men."

All of these things I wanted to tell Alice's father, wondered if
he would understand, if he would view me once again with
coolness and disdain, but not with hostility. I wanted to tell him,
also, how I felt after having lost the contest, having been denied a
chance at moving on to the regional level, then to the national,
and a possible college scholarship. I wanted him to know that, afterward, having received my fifteen dollars, third-prize consolation
check, I had walked outside the school down by the railroad
tracks, away from the sympathetic words of caring students, down
near the spot where they were laying foundations for new city
housing, among the weeds, across from patches of land covered by
small two-story houses. Here and there, a dog lay on the front
stoop and beautiful, Black children played in the backyards near

ripening watermelons, husky ears of corn, and little rows of peas, strung symmetrically upon silken thread—almost ready to bloom.

The children paid no attention to me, continued dwelling in their make-believe world. I was a stranger, almost an adult, and they had no idea of my anxieties, my fears. Like children, they were unable to recognize their anxieties. What did it matter to them that I smashed my fists into my hands, kicked at stones, that my breathing became strained, my nose filled with mucus, the tears streaming down my face? The world was, to them, the watermelon patch, and they did not yet know that there were weeds that could poison and kill. I wanted to reach out to them and to tell them that one day they would have to desert the land of peas and watermelons, to walk out among the barbarians. I longed to warn them to prepare for it, to arm themselves for it because they were Black, and poor, not mulatto. The dangers would confront them in triplicate. I walked past them: Why should I warn them? They would soon enough learn these things, soon enough come to know disappointments, the horror of living. Leave them, I averred, through reddened eyes, to their fairyland. Let them be happy if happy they are, while they can. I continued walking down the railroad tracks, finally rested upon a big rock, sat staring until late in the evening at the sky.

I could not, of course, tell Alice's father these things; they would not get me back into his tolerably good graces. Sitting there in his tweed jacket, smoking his pipe, he seemed oblivious to my presence, arrogant and contemptuous of the fact that I had taken it upon myself to sit down on one of the soft chairs. I knew that he, too, was the enemy, was part of the very class arrayed against those like me. I wouldn't admit it then, but I admired him, even in contrast to my own father. I wanted to be like him.

I was relieved when Alice appeared at the foot of the stairs. She said something to her father, who grunted but did not look in my direction, took my arm, and led me to the swing on the porch outside.

"Miss Frazier was by here today," she said, seating herself beside me. "She said you were a candidate for vice-president of the student council and it would be a bad mark on the school if you won. She said you were a smart aleck and a troublemaker and nobody but the rabble would vote for you. I said that I would vote for you too. My mother told me to shut up, but I told her that Miss Frazier wasn't telling the truth, that the only teachers and students who didn't like you were the jealous ones, and that Miss Frazier didn't like you because you were smart, and dark-skinned." She paused, as if embarrassed, but continued, "My daddy hit the ceiling, got mad, started shouting at me and made me go to my room. But I'm glad I said it."

I remained silent, pushed the swing back and forward, thought about writing a poem, a short story. If I could sit at the kitchen table for the rest of my life and write, no one would bother me. I would be able to get away from all the teachers, the madonna, my father, would be able to say the things I felt, find out what I really felt. I could make my own world and let no one against my choosing intrude.

Alice wanted me to reply, but I had nothing to say about running for the vice-presidency. I was even surprised about the nomination and knew that if successful, I would win. After the oratorical contest, many of the students had lined up even more strongly for me and against the faculty, particularly the Black students who, like Alice, sensed the reasons for my difficulty. I offered a condescending reply and quickly changed the subject.

"I finished the play," I said.

"How does it end?"

"Well, after mathematics and science are tried by the court, the judge rules that they are both important. That's how it ends."

"I don't think it should end that way. Science is more important than mathematics; you ought to have a jury find science the winner."

"That's what Copernicus says in his speech to the jury; but Bacon says that without mathematics there would be no science. So nobody wins and nobody loses."

The answer did not please her, though she remarked, "I think it's a good play." I thought so too, repeated the title, silently, *Mathematics versus Science*. After working so hard on it, I had felt good after finishing it, had even made copies and distributed them to my father, the principal, Alice, a few friends. I had written the play as a project for the Math and Science Club, of which both Alice and I were members. I know now, though, I had written it also in defense of myself, trying to point out to the hostile teachers that I was as smart as I had intimated, that I alone, could write a three-act play. I expected grudging admiration from them, not a cessation of hostilities. I didn't relish an uneasy truce; in fact, I somehow enjoyed the antagonism. The play was meant to make them notice me. The added resentment was unexpected. I did not realize how pervasive their antagonistic feelings toward me were, or how insecure they were concerning their own educational limitations, Like white people, they would tolerate no "smart alecky nigger."

The full extent of their animosity and pettiness came the following week, when the principal summoned me to his office. A teak-colored man, he was tall, bald-headed and nicknamed "Long John" and "Clean Head" by the students. He had a reputation for sending students home as a means of punishment, though he had never sent home any of the mulattoes. The vain hope I had nurtured that he had wanted to congratulate me about my play was dashed when, clearing his throat, he scowled at me from across the desk and said, "I'm forbidding you from running as an officer in the student council. I have a letter here signed by some of our teachers, and I concur with that letter. I don't think you're fit to represent the students of this school."

"What have I done?" I asked defensively.

"You know that better than I do."

"Who wrote the letter?" I asked, not expecting an answer.

"Boy," he bristled, almost coming out of his seat, "I don't have to explain anything to you. I've told you what I have to tell you. You're dismissed!"

Immobilized by his abrupt manner, his anger, I rose slowly, hesitantly from the chair, wanted to strike him, then remembered that I had sent him a copy of the play, wanted to remind him of it. "Did you read my play?" I asked, somewhat arrogantly.

"I read *a* play," he said, denying me even this triumph. "You sure you didn't copy it from somewhere?"

Defeated, now, meekly, I replied, "No, I didn't copy it, I wrote it."

He grunted, turned from me, began writing something on a piece of paper, looked up at me, still standing before his desk, growled, "I told you that's all; you're dismissed."

Leaving school, and walking down by the railroad tracks, I knew that I would have to leave Huntington; yet I would not give the teachers the satisfaction of knowing that they had defeated me, broken me, by dropping out of school altogether. With only one year left to go, I could transfer to Phenix High School in Hampton, Virginia, travel the thirty-odd miles by hitchhiking. I would have to explain my departure to Alice, my mother, and my father, but that did not matter so much. I knew that I would never be able to explain my real reasons for leaving, did not then really comprehend them myself. In time, however, I would discover that the almost total hostility of the faculty toward me was as much my fault as theirs. Like that of the madonna and some of the neighbors, their animosity toward me had little to do with personality, with me personally, but with the fact that I so desperately did not want to be what I was supposed to be. The more I read and the more I imagined becoming a writer, which I thought would impress people, and command respect, the more I drifted away from prescribed, determined roles. Even the madonna and some of my relatives called me strange, different; the madonna, in fits of rage, prophesied that I would end up in the electric chair, or come to a similar bad end. It was not for crimes committed, therefore, that animosity was directed toward me, but instead, because I had served notice that I was going to move outside of prescribed patterns, though in doing so I still sought to gain entry into the select class of "the better people of the community."

It was not from the better people of the community, however, that I received notice, attention, encouragement, but from the outcasts: the pimps and hustlers. The day after my altercation with the principal, ashamed to go back to school, I had gone up to Brown's poolroom and been met at the door by Red Drag, a tall, cream-colored pimp, with a cigarette drooping perpetually from his lips. The first time I had met Red Drag, I remembered, four years before, was while coming from a movie with Ollie and Horace. He had sauntered over from a discussion with some other pimps, put his hands on my shoulder, leading me away from my friends. "I hear you a smart little sonofobitch," he said softly.

Glowing with pride, wishing that Ollie and Horace could hear, I replied, "Oh, I'm all right."

"Looka here," he went on. "Now I want you to do me a favor." He looked over his shoulder. Satisfied that no one else was within earshot, he continued, "I ain't never learned to read and write. Like, I've been a hustler since I was old enough to beg for a bottle, so I ain't learned to read or write. Now, I want you do to me a favor, but don't you tell nobody, you hear, don't you tell nobody."

Red Drag had no way of knowing that I was too flabbergasted to tell anybody. Besides feeling a sense of pride that the number one pimp on the street knew about me, enough to consider me smart, enough to want me to teach him something, I was also saddened that this adult man could not read or write. I felt immense sympathy for him, and averted my eyes in order not to show him my compassion. He was assured I would tell no one.

"Okay," he said, "I'll let you know when I get some time, then we can start." He gave me a dime and went back to join his friends.

Brimming with satisfaction, I sauntered back to my friends, invented a conversation for their curiosity, between Red and myself, wanting to rush home right away and begin thinking of ways to teach someone to read and write, already imagining how good I would feel when Red read and wrote his first words, hoping that he would soon find time for us to begin.

He never found time, however. The next week he was picked up by the police, and when he came out of jail, he was wounded in a fight with a sailor. Now and then, I would meet him and ask him if he was ready, but he would disappoint me, give me a quarter or a dime, say he would let me know. Sometimes I would see him in the poolroom, looking over the shoulders of the other pimps at a paper or magazine, making facial expressions as if he too were reading, and one time he carried a letter around in his pocket from his home in Arkansas for a week, until he found me and asked me to read it to him. I felt sorry for him, but helpless also. I think he had given up the idea of ever learning to read and write.

Now, as I entered the poolroom, he put his hand on my shoulder, said, "Why ain't you in school?"

"My mother wanted me to stay home and do something for her," I lied.

He looked at me, skeptically. "You ain't in no trouble, is you, got kicked out of school?"

"No," I answered, "it's like I told you."

"All right," he said finally, "but you got to stay in school; if I find out you got kicked out, I'm gon kick your ass. Sure wished I had went, but I ain't even seen the first grade." He hugged me around the shoulder, and I almost told him what had happened at

Huntington, but thought that it was too late, now, to go back on the partial lie I'd already told.

"Ain't that your daddy, working at old Siegel's pawnshop over town?" He asked.

Ashamed, I answered in the affirmative.

He did not notice my embarrassment or shame, could not detect from my eyes, the contempt I held for my father. He said, "That ain't no job for a man smart as your daddy; them white folks screwed him, boy. If he was white, he'd be running some organization or something. Hell, he oughta get out of this damn town, go where a man can use his brains. Sweeping up that damn peck's store ain't no job for no educated man like him."

I nodded my head in agreement. I too wished my father would go away, would not remain here as a constant embarrassment to me, go away and maybe come back after having accomplished something big, become like Alice's father, respected and feared, be better able to protect me from the teachers. Now he could hardly protect himself. Ever since Pauline died and the Party could not get him a license to practice law, he spent most of his spare time whoring and drinking, respected among no one, except the pimps and prostitutes.

I was relieved when Tillie, one of the prostitutes who lived across the street in front of the poolroom, called out to Red, "Tell sweetmeat to come up here soons you finish with him, Red; I want him to go to the store for me," because I was able to terminate the discussion about my father.

Tillie, Black, short hair, big busts and behind, looked like Clarissa, and whenever I saw her I thought of Clarissa, became depressed because Clarissa died a year ago from tuberculosis. "Sweetmeat," Tillie said as I bounded through the door, "go over to Jew Balser's store and tell him to send me two steaks, some sauce, and a quart of beer and put it on my bill."

When I got outside, she hollered for me to bring her a pack of cigarettes.

By the time I returned from the store, Tillie had changed from tight-fitting men's pants, to a housecoat, that opened up the middle whenever she walked. She took the bags from my arms, motioned me to sit, said, "Why ain't you in school?"

I told her the lie I told Red Drag.

"How that pretty girl friend of yours?"

"Alice is all right."

"Just all right?" She winked at me. "When you gon finish school?"

"Next year."

"That's good. You gon be a politician like your daddy?"

"No, I'm going to be a writer."

"That's good, you gon be like Richard Wright?"

"Yes," I replied, somewhat enthusiastically, remembering the novel I had been trying to write. At night, when my sister and I had finished washing the dinner dishes, I sat at the kitchen table, writing on my tablet, tearing up pages and starting all over again. This coming summer, when I hoped to be working at Jew Balser's grocery store, I intended to buy a typewriter.

". . . you start writin them books," Tillie had continued, "and you come back and see old Tillie . . . I got some stories to tell you just won't wait . . . You want a beer?"

I said yes, but recoiled from her slightly as she opened it, brought it to me, cupped my chin in her hands.

She pulled my bowed head up so that my eyes met hers, laughed. "Oh, you so shy. What kinda sweetmeat is you? Don't you know how to look at a girl?"

I was looking at her and we both knew it, looking at the split in her housecoat, the fold of her panties around her large thighs; inside my pants, I had begun to stiffen. Bringing her face near mine, she kissed me on the lips, hard; I put my arms around her neck, stiffened more as she slid into my lap, the housecoat falling away to one side. "I bet when you a big-time writer, you won't even think about Tillie no more . . . but Tillie ain't no tramp. Tillie do what she got to do. Like your daddy workin in that pawnshop. That's what he got to do. He ain't no hustler, can't beat nobody outa no money, but he a colored man and he do what he got to do . . . but you smart, you go to school and you be uh writer; you kin do it if you want to. You got some brains up there and that's somethin them old pecks can't take from you."

I think, sympathetically now, that I should have given Tillie a copy of my play; yes, given one to her and Red Drag and the other pimps and prostitutes who liked me, befriended me. Even if they did not read it, could not understand it, they would have praised me for writing it, would have felt honored that I had given them a copy. Tillie stood, looked at her watch, took me by the hand, pulled me toward the bedroom: "C'mon, I'm gon give you somethin for going to the store."

Once inside the large bedroom, equipped with two chairs, a long table, plaid drapes, and a shaggy rug, she pulled back the covers on the bed, untied her robe, winked at me coquettishly.

"When you gon take off your clothes?" she asked, as I stood transfixed, stiffening inside of myself, staring at the curve of her body, the tight panties clinging to her large buttocks, the mounds of flesh peeping out across her brassiere. Embarrassed, I began to remove my clothes, turning my back to her. I had never done it with my clothes off before, not since Clarissa, when I was a little boy.

"You ain't never had no girl before, is you, sweetmeat?" she asked.

I threw back my head, laughed loudly, tried to make my words sound convincing. "Of course I have. Yeah, I have." Stripped down to my shorts, I moved toward the bed, tried to get on top of her, was rebuffed. "Whoa, boy!" Laughter. "Where you goin so fast? Don't you know that ain't no way to love a woman?" She cupped my face in her hands, kissed me hard on the lips, moved my hands to her breasts, guided them along the sides of her body, to the place between her legs, put her tongue into my ear, guided my face toward one of her large breasts.

I closed my eyes, hesitated, remembered: Tillie was a prostitute, and I had seen the white men with her in the cars—sometimes down on their knees, in the back seat, their head between her legs. I had heard that sometimes prostitutes made men go down on them, especially young men, and I thought that I was doing something wrong, that I should not be here. Still, I took her breasts in my mouth, began to suck hard, harder; guiding my face she moved it from one breast to the other, began to groan, to moan, and I remembered other groans and other moans, and remembered lying on the cot in the kitchen, taking myself in my hands, rubbing to the sound of the groans, the moans, feeling the soft, sticky liquid ooze out onto my shorts, the bed, lay ashamed, exhausted, wanting to shut out the groans, now, the moans.

The moans became short gasps of pleasure, whistles, and I am emboldened, almost pleasurably enraged, want them to continue, louder, am delighted with her seeming helplessness, want to fill the air with her screams, her crying. On my own, now, I moved my hands across, up and down her body, her stomach, her long legs, eased down her panties, ran my hands softly around the crotch between her legs, pressed my face full force upon her breasts, moved with abandon now, creating my own sense of rhythm, touching all the spots she had manuevered me to before, entered her, heard the scream, then the soft whimper, smiled as a, yes, conqueror might smile, remembered the sounds of another bedroom, and hating her and loving her at the same time, wanting to call her name, as she called mine, as the madonna called the others, and feeling ashamed too, and wanting to die, sensing that I was doing something wrong, that the madonna would hate me for it, and my father would hate me for it too, but feeling exhilarated, happy, and wanting the screaming and the noise to go on, even though I was ashamed, and wanted to die . . .

Two days later, on a visit to my father, I carried around still the conflicting feelings of bravado and guilt. I felt an assurance of manhood at the fact that I had seduced Tillie (how was I to understand then, that I was the seduced, instead), had made her happy, had drawn favorable comments from her about my lovemaking. But the shame and the guilt were there too, and I hid as much as possible from my mother, believing, somehow, that even after washing prodigiously, if I came too close to her, she would smell the smell of Tillie, become enraged, chastise me.

I avoided coming too close to my father for the same reason, believed that the smell of Tillie lingered still. After greeting him, I moved hastily to the sofa. He was angry with me. There was no hint of this on his impassive face, but I knew it—felt it. He had been drinking, was slightly drunk, yet he did not let down his guard, did not reveal the way he felt about anything. I sat, waiting for him to speak, marveling at the fact that I no longer feared him, was ashamed that I had even developed something of contempt for him. I had not been able to see him over these past years without comparing him to those like Alice's father, without believing that, in becoming an alcoholic, a porter, he had betrayed not himself so much, but me, could not help but believe, too, what would become clearer in later years, that he was guilty of having deserted me, having left me alone, with no resources, no real guidance, left me incapable of dealing with the madonna.

I was to realize later, also, that this was one of the reasons I sought intellectual arguments with him, challenging him often to refute him, trying to break down his armor of self-assurance, to best him in that area in which he held the greatest measure of respect: his mind, the intellect. I wanted, I suppose, to demolish him here, best him here, and thus reduce him to something less than a man.

The whiskey, however, had not dulled his mind; he remained as sharp and agile as ever, fixed his eyes upon me, let his words roll out in measured tones. "So you're leaving Huntington and going to Phenix! And you didn't tell me. Rainey [the assistant principal, whom I liked] has to tell me that my boy is running away."

He was angry, I thought, because I did not tell him, but also because I did not come to him for help, that I took things into my own hands. I was not yet so independent of him that I could confront him directly, say what came to my mind. I did not then tell him that I did not come to him because I knew that he could do nothing, that his old power was gone, that a father who swept floors would embarrass me by appealing to the principal on my behalf.

Instead, I said, "They hate me at Huntington; they won't let me graduate."

"I thought you said that Mrs. Green liked you, that Mr. Rainey liked you, Mr. Johnson . . . Rainey says it's true that some of the teachers are against you, but not everybody . . . not everybody . . ."

"Some of them are all right, but they can't do anything. Mr. Rainey—he can't do anything if they won't let me graduate, and I don't want them to; I'll do things for myself."

He winced slightly, but recovered quickly, hiding the anger in his voice. "Boy, the world is not like that. People need each other, especially colored people. The people sometimes don't know it themselves. But that's the way this country is. The big men who run things try to make people think they don't need each other, that they're rugged individualists. They keep people divided that way—Blacks from whites, poor Blacks from other Blacks; but poor people need each other." He paused, reflected, continued, "Suppose you opened a store and you got all the goods you needed— meat, fruit, vegetables, that kind of stuff. You still need customers, because if you don't have customers, you might as well not have a store. That's how much people need each other—like a store owner needs a customer and a customer needs a store owner."

"I don't need the people at Huntington," I said. "Most of them are Uncle Toms—you said so yourself."

"I didn't say you shouldn't try to understand them because they're Uncle Toms. Most colored people and white people too are Uncle Toms of one sort or another, whether they know it or not. Most of them don't know it. . . . You keep talking about Richard Wright, well, one thing about a writer is that he has to understand even the people he doesn't like, because he knows that this system does things to make people do things they wouldn't do if they were free."

The part about the writer stung, and I knew that he must be right, that a writer must be able to understand people, that like or dislike, hatred or love, had very little to do with understanding, but I was not ready to concede my father this small victory. "Why should I understand somebody who hates me, whom I hate?" I asked.

"You don't know if they hate you or not. Maybe they don't. They might be jealous of you or scared of you, threatened by you. That's different from hate. Anyway, for you to hate them makes no sense. That way you can't deal with them, can't even understand what they're doing to you. That way you run away, you don't fight, and when you start running, you don't stop so easily."

He was angry and I know now what I could not clearly understand then, that this anger was different from the anger of years back. A few years before, the anger would have resulted in him issuing forth a torrent of words, overwhelming me with them, his finger jabbing in my direction, the tone now arrogant, now cajoling; after the lecture I would be summarily dismissed, not allowed to present, not daring even to attempt to present, my own case. Now he at least listened, had been listening for the past two years (was it because he now considered me almost an intellectual equal, or because he was growing older?), and his anger now was not so arrogant, so threatening. I was glad to see the anger now, happy to see the old fire come back to his eyes, watch him groping, reflecting, searching for the conclusive phrase, the demolishing last word. Did he know then, what I could not clearly comprehend at that time, that the debates between us brought us together, enabled us to reach one another, and that the anger, his and mine, served to remind us both that we were eternal warriors, destined to engage in combat, for whatever spoils we did not know?

". . . You don't think they'll let you graduate," he came back at me. "So what? Is it worth running away just to graduate? If you run away just to graduate, you'll know all of your life that you ran away. The people at that school have power, I know that. The white folks gave it to them. But that don't mean that you don't fight that power; even if they don't let you graduate, or even if they could kill you, you fight—because if you don't, it makes it easier for them to use that power to hurt somebody else."

Drunk or not, the old power shone through—the quickness of mind, of intellect, the oratorical skills, and as always when confronting him, listening to him, watching him, the contrast between him and those like Alice's father became blurred. In retrospect, I realize that what I admired in him, respected in him, went far deeper than skin color or status. There was about him a subtlety which bespoke worlds which I could only imagine, worlds accessible only through the magic of words and intellect, where men met on the common ground of knowledge, devoid of such considerations as skin color, status, wealth, worlds conceivable by writers, philosophers, and saints, where I imagined I would feel most comfortable. They were worlds of loneliness, of isolation, for such wares—quickness of mind and intellect—were, in that Virginia town, not marketable, were regarded with aversion and contempt. For me, of course, the world was Newport News, Virginia, and I suspected that what held true here, must hold elsewhere, that those like my father would forever be outcasts, outside the community of man, while those like Alice's father would always be welcomed, respected, admired. Alone with him, trying to follow his words, to counteract them, trying to match him with quick thinking, I felt as I did when sitting in the kitchen, writing late at night at the table—I would have liked to remain, forever, talking, listening, learning. There was, however, a world outside to which I was more than attracted, and once away from my father, that world loomed more and more important, and the old contempt for him would invariably return. I would be ashamed of his job, of his drinking, regretful that I did not have a father such as the mulattoes had.

CHAPTER 3

Though Alice, my father, and mother may have protested against my leaving Huntington High School to go to Phenix, the teachers at Huntington seemed somewhat relieved. Their hostility, though as pronounced as ever, was tempered by the fact that they believed they had won, had scored a victory over the smart aleck. They did not really believe that I would continue my education, I suppose. Perhaps they thought I would drift over the summer months, as so many did, into work at the shipyard.

They had no idea, however, of how intensely I hated them, how much I wanted to avenge myself upon them. They couldn't have understood that their animosity toward me was a challenge that propelled me not to become a dropout. They made me more determined than ever to graduate from school, to strike back at them.

They did not believe me when I boasted to other students that I was writing a novel. How could they have even guessed that the plot sequence of the novel constructed in my imagination, showed a character, me, pitted against the world, them, and that I emerged victorious? The novel began to take shape during the summer, when I bought a second-hand typewriter and first with one finger, then with two, began to write almost daily. I would go to my summer job as a clerk at Jew Balser's store, return home, drag out my typewriter, and begin to write. Usually, on the weekends, I would go out with Laura (Alice's parents had sent her away for the summer), who was spending the three-months vacation in Newport News, with her aunt.

Laura, seventeen, one year younger than me, was from North Carolina. She was light-complexioned, though her skin seemed redder than that of the mulattoes in Newport News, her hair was bobbed about her head, and her large laughing eyes were the most distinctive feature about her. I met Laura while working in the store, saw her come in day after day, hesitated about saying much to her, yet always hurried to wait on her. One day, not expecting an affirmative answer, I asked her, half-heartedly, to go out with me. To my surprise, she laughed, accepted, consented to let me take her to "the garden."

It was not a garden in the real sense of the word. No crops grew there—no watermelons, sweet peas, ears of corn, or butter beans. There were, however, long rows of trees standing side by side, tall and very green, along a cobblestoned walk and clusters of hedgerows, all with multicolored spiders, running up and down their trunks. There were flowers too; besides the wild dandelions, there were bright yellow buttercups and rich red roses, slightly bowed, their buds, like lovers, closed around each other. Tall, blazing, red tulips grew alone, glistening in the pureness of their own color, in the silence of a singular kind of majesty.

The garden, located between Hampton and Newport News, was situated in what had once been an all-white neighborhood. The entire area—almost three blocks of trees, flowers, park benches, and old, dull gray rocks, had once been part of an estate owned by a rich white man who, long ago, shortly before his death, had sold the property to the city. When Negroes began moving into the area during wartime, the whites began to move out. By the war's end, few whites remained. The trees, shrubbery and flowers were well tended, however, perhaps because of the few whites who did remain. Often I came here to write, to think, to be alone. Lately, I had begun to come each weekend, knowing that soon the white people who remained would move away and the city would either tear down the place or stop caring for it altogether.

"This is nice," Laura remarked laughingly as we walked close to each other, down the paved walkway. Her eyes sparkled, were bright, I believe, because she liked to laugh a lot. She offered her hand, and I hesitated, then took it somewhat reluctantly. She was talking and could not see my embarrassment, my fear even, did not feel my hand stiffen in hers. Laura could never know that, as she had moved her hand toward mine, like all the other times, with Alice, with the madonna, when real intimacy threatened, I would become panicky. I recall vaguely, fleetingly, the time I had approached the madonna, trying to take her face in my hands, to kiss her cheeks. With her palms upspread, she shoved me, ruthlessly, away from her, causing my books to drop to the floor, and I had gone to school and hidden in the bathroom until my eyes were no longer red . . .

". . . Everywhere you go," Laura continued, "the white people have the nice things; even in Rocky Mount." She paused, laughed. "Well, almost they got all the best things. But they don't know it and they don't have no fun with it. I bet if this park was colored people's there would be singing and dancing; we would've torn down them old nasty spiders and put up a jukebox and we'd be dancing. That's what we'd do in Rocky Mount."

I smiled, but said nothing, suspected that I would not like that, would not want Black people to have this garden, because I knew that she was right. If it belonged to us, there would be gaiety and happiness here, no matter that the people had nothing to be gay or happy about. But they would be happy, here, for a brief time, the girls kicking up their skirts and showing their legs, and the men fondling the girls, kissing them, sneaking a feel up their dresses. The children would be running, jumping, and shouting at the tops of their voices. There was peace and quiet here now, something that reminded me of a graveyard; this, I thought, was the way it should be.

". . . You a shy one, ain't you?" Laura said, laughing. "Why you so shy?"

"I'm not so shy."

"Sure you are, and you try to come on so sophisticated-like, but"—more laughter—"you so shy and bashful."

I grabbed her by the waist, turned her around, laughed, guided her to an open clearing on the grass, where we rolled together, tickling each other, laughing, and I was not so ashamed anymore that we were close together, touching, our bodies rolling off each other. We had pulled blades of grass up from the roots to put inside each other's clothes, we had been intimate, two Black children playing in the white people's garden, holding each other, laughing together.

Afterward, we lay on our backs, looking up at the sky, her hand in mine, and I felt peaceful, contented, knew that I liked her very much. I was not afraid of her, did not feel intimidated by her, the way that I had with most mulattoes, even with Alice. I knew that when she laughed it was not about the way I looked or the way I talked, not because I wrote poetry and was trying to write a novel, or because I wanted to be like Richard Wright. She would not, I believed, have laughed at me even if I had told her how angry I was most of the time, how frightened I was. Maybe she would have laughed, but I would know that she was not laughing at me.

I felt comfortable with Laura. During the next few weeks, I took her around the city, showing her Jefferson Avenue, the East End, even the backyard—that place where I grew up so fast, my grandmother said, during the last fourteen years. It is not only one yard, this backyard, but many, stretching nearly two miles from end to end. At one time there had been fences all along the block, separating the two-story houses. But over the years, the boys in the neighborhood—"yall holligans," according to my mother—had chopped down the fences and sold them to the neighbors for firewood. People would go to bed at night and wake up the next morning to discover their fence gone. Later that evening, the women would cook fried chicken and rice, or pig tails and beans, neckbones and black-eyed peas, ham hocks and collard greens, or pork chops and okra, on what had been, just the day before, somebody else's backyard fence.

Though I am not sure I successfully communicated it, I tried to tell Laura what the backyard meant to me, how, growing up here, I did not feel so afraid, was not so shy or withdrawn. I felt protected and loved and wanted and, despite our pranks, the people, men and women, thought of us all as part of a family who, like them, were placed here by God knows who or what. We were all making the best of things, sharing with each other, caring for each other, trying, as much as possible, to protect each other—attending the funerals of those who passed away, giving of our meager resources—each for the other's benefit.

Here, no child was allowed to be an outsider, regardless of what he might feel. Whatever the antagonisms between adults, chil-

dren belonged to all, protagonist and antagonist alike. Besides
poverty, children were people's visible possession. I told Laura of
some of these men and women, recalling them with a sense of
nostalgia, not yet able to understand, as I would much later, what
they had meant to me, how through their examples, they helped
to prevent me from falling into complete cynicism, enabled me to
look back, during the coming years of depression and sadness, and
recall a world not altogether cruel and brutal.

They were good people, these men and women. Mrs. Nelson,
short, Black, and skinny, who the neighbors said practiced roots,
was the only one whose fence had remained standing through all
the years. She used to give us cake and pie, which we had been
afraid to eat . . . Mr. Cufee, the deaf-mute, who worked in the
coal yard, stealing coal from his job to sell to the neighbors for
half price . . . Mr. Bentley, the man who boasted that he could
beat any man on the block, but was afraid of his wife, who out-
weighed him by almost a hundred pounds . . . Mrs. Ruby, who
had always shown up at funerals and birthdays, bringing condo-
lences and presents . . . Mr. Paxton, who once stood off two
policemen who had tried to make an arrest in his home without a
warrant . . . Mr. Anderson, who kept a big tin tub in his
woodhouse for making corn whiskey, pouring in the sugar and alcohol, sometimes adding grapefruit juice, then boiling it, stirring
it, and finally adding cherry juice to lend it color. We used to
watch him make it, in the backyard—he'd sometimes let us taste it.
I remember laughing as we pretended being drunk and staggered
all over each other . . .

I wanted to tell Laura, also, that during the week nights, when
I was finishing my novel or reading, I wrote poems about her, to
her. These must have been among the happiest days of my life, I
now recall. I would never be able to walk through the garden
again without remembering her. There were many other things
that I wanted to tell her, but soon the summer had ended and
she had gone back to North Carolina, leaving me with fond
memories and a notebook full of poems. I did not go down to the
train station to see her off, that Sunday of clouds and blue sky,
for the depression had set in two days before she was to leave.

The laughter during those final days was forced and strained,
lacking the spontaneity and exuberance of earlier times. I was unable to eat very much, did not sleep very well, was angry and

sharp with my sisters and mother. This upsetting state continued for about three weeks after Laura had gone, until one day when I received a letter from her. Only then did the depression begin to subside, and I began to feel less hostile, less lonely, less afraid.

By September, when I had begun my first semester at Phenix High School, I was in, for me, at least, a jovial state of mind. By then, I was nearing the completion of my novel and I was striking back at the teachers at Huntington High School by not dropping out of school. Because I no longer saw Alice at school each day, we grew apart, despite her return to the city. I did not become depressed, but thought of Laura and the summer instead and was not sorry that I visited Alice no longer. Mentally, therefore, I was unprepared for the shocking manner in which my mother announced to me, when I came home from school one evening, that my father had suffered a stroke. He was paralyzed.

There was something in the telling—the tone of her voice, the veiled, perhaps unrecognized innuendos, coupled with hints of satisfaction, if not glee—that the reaper had been paid, the sinner brought to the bar of final repentance. I know now that she was frightened, that she felt helpless, but I could only think then that, somewhere in the catalogue of her mind, she had run through the list of injustices enacted against her and gained sadistic satisfaction that he, the architect of so much misery in her life, had been brought so low. Because I had often been the recipient of such tales of injustice, as if somehow I too were guilty of having transgressed against her, I suppose I identified with my father in his prostrate condition. I believed that the avenging angel, having struck once on my mother's behalf, might strike again. I was angry therefore, at her tone, her manner, and I wanted to curse her, strike out at her. I became even more enraged when she identified her God as the avenging angel: "I guess he know there's a God, now. Just like you—always talkin about there ain't no God, don't believe in no God, but God don't love no ugly and now you see what God done and he see what God done."

How could I have known then how much her God meant to her, how much he meant to them all. It was only natural that he was the architect of fortune as well as disaster, that he was performing his duties if he rewarded you with the correct number for the day, or if he inflicted illness or misery upon an enemy. She took her God more seriously than I ever would have, believed in him as I never could have. If he was the Savior and avenging angel for her, he was for me, that one time when I seriously entered one of his tabernacles, the passport for romance with a girl who could only be approached through him.

My reason for joining Elder Michaux's Church of The Holy Ghost, when I was sixteen, unknown to my mother, was not because I had been suddenly converted, but only because I was attracted to Berniece, an ardent member with large thighs fitted to a well-rounded body. Failing to seduce her, I left the church almost as quickly as I had enrolled, to the consternation and hostility of my mother. No, I could not take this God of my mother's seriously, this white man. I felt contempt toward her for accepting him, for believing in him.

Yet my father had been struck down, rendered helpless. When they permitted me to see him, four days later, he was raised up in bed, staring about the antiseptic, white room—with the white night stand and the white walls, the assortment of flowers—like a man surprised, overwhelmed. There was an unfamiliar hollowness in his eyes, a relaxation of his body that seemed feigned. His left hand dangled uselessly at his side and the drooling from his mouth turned his nightgown a darkened gray. I spoke to him, asking him a series of questions; either he did not hear me or pretended not to. He just continued to sit, oblivious to my presence, staring off into space, while I lapsed into silence, wrung my hands, wanted to smash out at the white room, to smash out even at him.

I realize now, from the vantage point of so many years, that there were two victims in that room, on that day, not only him, but myself as well. My mother's avenging angel, in bringing my father so low, in rendering him so helpless, had robbed me of a significant victory, had denied me the chance at my own kind of vengeance. The antagonism between us, I had fancied, could be resolved only when I had learned enough and become mature enough to meet him on an equal footing, one intellectual to another, and I now often envisioned myself confronting him as he had often confronted me, terrorizing him with words, rendering all his answers, his arguments impotent. In my mind were stored the many debates I had lost to him, those which I had longed to avenge. One debate in particular, which had occurred some three years earlier and stuck out in my mind, concerned the lynching of a Black man in Gloucester County. . . .

The night after the lynching, on a makeshift stand highlighted by two ground lights and surrounded by the American flag and a crowd of people, Black and white—though few whites—my father had spoken of the necessity for Black men to defend themselves. In addition, however, he had reiterated his usual theme, admonishing the Blacks to join hands with the whites to combat capitalism, the real enemy. He had continued, arguing that both groups were victims of lynching by an economic and social system designed to force the poor to war against each other.

In his living room the next day, we had assumed our usual positions, he energetic, confident, pacing the floor, thumbs hooked like deadly weapons into his vest pockets, ready to spring forward in my direction whenever he had some telling point to make. I had sat on the sofa, trying to follow his bodily movements and his argument at the same time. Though the years of reading and writing had given me a fair vocabulary, I had sensed my inferiority, yet his willingness to even entertain arguments from me had demonstrated some small condescension to my talents. I knew then that I would never possess that storehouse of words that he had at his command, that even if I did, I would never be able to hurl them with such shotgun rapidity, never make them serve me as well as they served him.

The need to engage him in combat, however, had been so strong that I hastily took the initiative: "They keep lynchin us because we never do anything. We make speeches and talk about what we ought to do. But we don't ever do anything, and they'll keep lynchin us until we do something."

He had rocked back on his heels, a smile dancing across his face. "What do you think we should do?"

"Every time they kill a colored person, we ought to kill two white people. Every time they burn down a colored person's house, like they did in Suffolk that time, we ought to burn down two of theirs."

He shook his head, moved closer: "Which whites would you lynch, which ones' homes would you burn down?"

"Anybody's. It don't matter; anybody's; they all the same."

"Suppose they're innocent, suppose they didn't lynch anybody, don't like lynching, would like to do something about it."

"It doesn't matter; they won't stop unless we do something other than talk."

He had advanced upon me, stopping a few feet from the couch: "There is a difference between justice and revenge, a difference between revolution and nihilism. Do you know what nihilism is?"

And so round one was his because I did not know what nihilism was, and he had to explain it to me. "Nihilism is an irrational act, spontaneous, guided by no laws or principles, demanding no responsibility. It means to want to kill innocent people, not for justice, but for self-gratification. Any fool can be a nihilist. You don't have to think or plan, or act rationally, you just act."

Round two was his. He had demonstrated, without mentioning me, that I was what I did not want to be: an advocate or irrationality, an opponent of thought and reason. "You can't get justice in this country," I had lashed back, clearly on the defensive. "You said so yourself, and you don't have to be a nihilist to know that when it comes to us and white people, it's an eye for an eye and a tooth for a tooth."

Shrugging his shoulders, he had moved away from the couch, sauntered arrogantly toward the window. I had been on the ropes by then and he knew it. I had resorted to clichés—even biblical ones—out of desperation, as he had understood. I wanted to leave, to avoid the pummeling in store for me. Unmoving, however, I had remained, listening—spellbound.

"An eye for an eye is good for cave men. All things are equal to cave men. There is no equality here. White people outnumber us. They have all the guns; they have the laws and the prisons; they have an army. Now they even have an atomic bomb.

"Now, by ourselves, boy [the ultimate insult], the only thing we can do against that kind of power is get killed. But we can try to get some of those people with guns, some of those in the army, to understand that the lynchers are after them too, that the people who run this country, the money men, lynch them every day in many different ways. And when you do that you take care of the lynchers—the big ones and the little ones."

But I hadn't allowed myself to be disposed of so easily, had had to fight back from the ropes, refusing to allow him such an easy victory: "That won't happen. White people think they're better than us. They'll never do that. Them friends of yours, Mr. Kovaks and Mr. Larson: they wouldn't fight with us. No, the white people hate us, and I hate them too, and we have to kill them before they kill us." It was a desperate effort; my speech was almost incoherent and I knew that I had lost again, that the argument was over.

He had walked over to my side of the couch, fixing his eyes upon me. "You hate white people; but you don't know any white people. You know the ones you read about. As far as you know, there might be good ones as well as the others. But you say, 'Kill them all.' You don't know what that word means either. No one should kill out of hatred. That's what lynchers do. But human life is sacred. Those men you hate, and I hate them too, in a way, are victims of systems and institutions. That is what must be destroyed. Not people."

He had sat a while longer on the couch, and I had sensed a momentary tenderness about him. It was soon gone, however, and he became the cold, calculating warrior again. "I did not get you today," I had told myself, "but maybe the next time, and if not then, maybe the next."

But I never got him. Whatever the argument—communism, religion, books, Negroes—I ended up, head down on the sofa, feeling inferior, wanting him to touch me, to hold me, to caress me. He never did. After an emotional outburst from me, he might come close, sit beside me on the couch. Soon, however, he assumed his previous stance, becoming distant, analytical.

Here now, on this bed, in this antiseptically clean room, he appeared neither distant, analytical, nor calculating. The voice, once powerful, was stilled, the once vibrant energetic body, dysfunctional. From the penetrating eyes which he closed again and again —tears? Yes, tears, and I almost dashed from my seat in surprise. I don't recall ever having seen him cry before. My mother, yes, all the time. Tears were her weapons as words had been his, and with them she moved her household, propelled her children into action, bringing us down to her level, forcing us to do the impossible for her sake. But tears were antithetical to my father's makeup, the warning sign that something had happened to throw his world into disarray. There was something out there that he could not cope with, that overwhelmed him. I wanted to hold him in my arms, to wipe away the tears, even to kiss him, but I could not. I could not even move any closer to his bed, could not wipe the tears from his cheek. All that I could do was rise silently to leave in sorrow, disgust, and helplessness.

Altogether, my father remained in the hospital and a special nursing home for almost three months. He had lost the use of the entire left side of his body. On one of my visits, when he was undergoing therapy, the aides were teaching him to walk with a cane, using one side of his body to propel the lifeless other. His mental faculties remained unimpaired, though his voice was no longer powerful, strong, threatening; instead, he spoke more slowly, with more control, his voice lacking intonation. We did not argue very much on my infrequent visits, primarily, I suppose, because he always had a number of other visitors. The pimps and prostitutes came to visit, as well as members of the Party, Black and white, and a few of his girl friends. Absent among the list of visitors was my mother, who, perhaps remorseful over her former remarks, now preferred not to hear of him or discuss him. When she knew that I had visited him, she would ask me how he was, then quickly move toward another conversation.

On the occasions when we were alone, I told him about Phenix High School, and my experiences there, completely different from those I had undergone at Huntington. I told him that the class and caste distinctions so pronounced at Huntington were not visible there, that there was at Phenix among poor and middle-class students, among Blacks and mulattoes a sense of comradeship, even of caring. Blacks and mulattoes dated here without censure or disapproval of the faculty, who themselves, both Black and mulatto, went out of their way to help and encourage students. When the dramatics teacher discovered that I liked to write, she wanted to see my writings, had read a part of my novel, and commented upon it. I was asked to join the drama club and had been given star roles, like the narrator in *Our Town*; and the defense attorney, in a play, whose title, I no longer recall. When one of the teachers discovered that I lived in Newport News, usually hitchhiking to school, he contacted a friend who taught at Hampton Institute, a short distance away, who also lived in Newport News. The teacher persuaded him to bring me out to Hampton on those days when he taught his classes.

I had no doubt that the teachers would allow me to graduate, and I began to fantasize about the coming event, often marching around the neighborhood to the tune of "Pomp and Circumstance," thinking of the victory I would win over the faculty at Huntington, gloating about it.

I told my father these things in order to justify my having left Huntington High School, to remove the stigma of "having run away," though he seemed not to have relented in his former appraisal. He didn't once tell me that I had done the best thing. I did not tell him, however, that even at Phenix High, I felt an outsider, despite the sincerity, warmth, and comradeship of the teachers and students. It was not, I know now, that they did not accept me, but that I could not completely accept them, believed always, unconsciously, that I would discover their warmth as ungenuine, that at some point they would reveal another side of themselves, and attempt to humiliate me, to laugh at me. I was still attracted to the mulattoes, to those like Alice's father and Alexander. Though ingratiation was not necessary, I still condescended toward them, made friends with them, visited their homes, so different in attitude from those I had visited in Newport News. I still longed for the day when I might become like them.

The wish to become like them seemed more intensified. For the first time in her life, my mother became incapable of work, and we were again forced upon the welfare rolls. I had to contend with the pompous white woman in the conservative blue suit who, on her monthly visits to us, fidgeted uncomfortably on the edge of her seat. Terrified of roaches, which I knew she had never seen, she asked me constantly about my grades, the forthcoming graduation, reminding me that after graduation I was expected to go to the shipyard, to support my mother.

The humiliation was pronounced and so was the rage, but it was a rage that could be expended only when I was alone, walking through the garden—I could not tell the white woman what I felt, what I thought—or what I wrote in poems late at night. My visits to the homes of my mulatto classmates, now as before, only intensified my shame, my embarrassment, forcing me to make unfair comparisons between my parents and theirs, forcing me to unleash part of my rage against my mother, with an almost outward show of contempt for my father.

The contempt was evidenced when I visited him two weeks after he had been released from the hospital and one week after I had given him the novel I had completed. Handing him the manuscript to read, I recalled the night of its completion, remembered slumping across the kitchen table as I imagined Richard Wright might do, then, rising, holding my hands over my head, wanting to shout to the entire neighborhood that I had written a novel. I had tossed and turned on my couch all night, unable to sleep, already imagining myself a recognized writer, seeing the people who condescended toward me—who respected me. I remembered showing it to my mother in the morning, the next-door neighbor, my teachers, to whom I promised a copy (a promise I never fulfilled); I told my fellow students about it, told Red Drag and Tillie, called Alice for the first time in four months, told her, hoping that she would tell her father. I wanted to call every teacher at Huntington and tell them. Having given the manuscript to my father to read—my only, badly-typed copy—I was unable to reread it at night, and forced to reconstruct the plot sequence in my mind, often falling asleep while doing so.

Over three hundred pages long, the book was entitled *Fear Not, Young Blood*. The major characters were Larry (white, handsome, bluish-black hair, blue eyes) and Joy (mulatto, pretty, creamy-white skin, blue eyes). The plot centered around Joy. Born in the slums, she was a child prodigy, able to read and write at the age of five, capable of doing college work at the age of fifteen. She completed medical school at the age of twenty-one, and soon became renowned as a surgeon, respected and admired throughout the world. Larry is also a famous surgeon, and the two meet and fall in love. Soon afterward, Joy contracts an eye disease, is blinded. She does not want to give up her profession, hoping to continue her role as a surgeon. She is rebuffed by the medical association when she pleads to be allowed to continue performing operations. After many such pleas, the association decrees that if she can prove her surgical competence, her appeal will be approved. Joy needs a guinea pig, someone who will entrust his life to a blind surgeon. In the final pages of the novel, Larry plunges a knife into his abdomen, providing his love with a patient. The novel ends with Joy about to perform the operation.

Expecting my father to be as enthusiastic about the book as I was, expecting praise, I was therefore surprised when, almost immediately after I had greeted him, having returned one week after giving him the manuscript, he calmly asked, "Why do you want to be white?"

I raised my hands, as if warding off some unforeseen blow,

dropped the smile from my face, walked over to the little alcove which served him as a kitchen, and said, with obvious hostility, "Why do you think I want to be white?"

He had underlined parts of the novel and he now read them to me, concluding, "The only Blacks in this book are the servants of Larry and Joy. Joy has no parents; she is brought up in a white orphanage; so is Larry. No, there are no Black people."

I sat, looking about the room, letting the silence descend around us. He was wrong, I knew, but I could not then explain to him how wrong he was. Not in his descriptions, no, for in this book, black skin was at a minimum, thick lips and kinky hair nonexistent. But this was not, I knew, because I wanted to be white. I knew no white people beyond those I had done some work for, or those whom I had read about. No, he was wrong on that score, and I have often wondered if during those years before his death, he had ever calculated how wrong he was, if he ever, like me, came to realize that my desire was not to be white, but to be mulatto. But how could he have then known what I only surmised— that Larry was modeled upon Alice's father and me, that Joy was modeled upon the women who most attracted me?

His implication was that I was attempting to lose my identity, to deny my heritage. But of the reality of my identity, I knew little, having so often imagined myself, out of shame, to be other than I was. As for my heritage, whatever that was had been determined by mulattoes, who had made the great contributions— Booker T. Washington, Frederick Douglass, George Washington Carver. Even Richard Wright was not Black like me. How could I have known then, that almost on the eve of my graduation from high school, I had come close to resolving the conflict within my own breast? Reason, thinking, knowledge were not ends in themselves, ends which would leave me, like my father, defeated, poverty-stricken, dreamless, but means toward another end: power, respect, admiration. Having not been born mulatto, I could only approach these ends through the route he had so often prescribed, but I could only avenge myself upon others by attaining the other ends.

Leaving him later that night, when conversation between us, due to my undisguised hostility, became impossible, I was broken, defeated. This was not because of the charges that he had made, but because he intimated that the book was not a good one, tell-

ing me that I should write about the things that I knew, adding
that I could ask Saunders Redding, a writer on the staff of Hampton Institute, to read it for me, get another opinion. I went home,
took my typewriter from the closet, covered it, put it away in my
mother's room, sealed the manuscript in an envelope to put it out
of sight, and tried not to fantasize about becoming famous any
longer, tried instead to think of my coming graduation, now only
two months away.

I was somewhat relieved three weeks later, though, when
Saunders Redding, who had agreed to read my manuscript, wrote,
"You have something to say, and one day you will say it. As for
now, you must read as much as you can and experience as much
as you can." My depression was not much eased. The vehicle that
I had thought would raise me above my condition, enable me to
wreak vengeance upon my enemies, pointing out to them that I
was not a failure, had not worked. And perhaps, I thought, they
were right. I was a failure, and no matter the effort, would always
be one. Writing and publishing a novel would have been the
quickest and most dramatic way of arousing them, of having them
sit up and take notice of me, and this I was unable to accomplish.
Once again, I felt rage, but felt also unable to expend it, to find a
suitable target for it. Due, perhaps, to these dual, conflicting feelings, I was not altogether unhappy when, a few days after receiving Redding's note, I tried to kill Walter.

Walter was as close to being white as one could come, without
being so. He was an albino, yet the other mulattoes treated him
with disdain, as somewhat of a freak. Everything about him was
white—his hair, his face, legs, even the hair on his arms. Until he
had been disowned by the mulattoes, I had treated him with a
measure of condescension, but seeing that he was not considered
among the elite of the Newport News mulatto class, I had started
ignoring him. On those few occasions when I would go to the recreation center—a center established for Black youth, not far from
my home, I would encounter Walter, sometimes argue with him.

Arguments among teen-agers at the recreation center took the
form of "rags," where one made insulting, derogatory remarks
about one's opponent, hoping to draw laughter from the audience. Because of my vocabulary and my quickness with words, I
was good at "ragging," and Walter was among my favorite targets. Comments by me, which were frequently directed toward his

weird appearance, his slowness in school, his inability to find and hold a girl friend, usually drew continuous laughter from others, and forced him to retreat in humiliation. Whatever our fight was about on that night, I do not now know, but my constant ragging him, I am sure, had something to do with it.

Yet, when he put his arms around me after I had walked into the center that night, and guided me outside, I had no idea that a fight would ensue. Not overly surprised at his behavior, I assumed he was attempting to ingratiate himself with me. Once outside, however, when we had moved a few feet from the center, he struck me upon the head, momentarily dazing me, the blow forcing me to my knees, where I tried to fight off the bright flashes of light and an interminable period of darkness.

I recovered from the darkness, groped, made my way toward a construction sight nearby and armed myself with the heaviest bricks I could find. I cursed and cried each step of the way; the bricks felt gritty beneath my arms, in my hands. I entered the center. When I saw Walter glancing apprehensively at the door, I heaved a brick with all my strength and caught him in the stomach. He doubled over. I cursed loudly; the tears and mucus tasted salty in my mouth. I released another brick, aiming this time for his forehead. The brick found its mark and brought forth a long stream of blood. He fell to the floor, prostrate. I advanced upon him, raised a brick over the top of my head, coiled my arms, was poised for the kill, moved closer, closer . . .

I wanted to move close enough to feel his hurt, taste it, revel in it; I wanted to see him suffer. Out of the darkness of the rage of yesterday and today, there was seemingly a voice shouting, "Kill him, kill him!" and I realized that I wanted not only to kill him, but to destroy him, to obliterate him. I kicked him hard in the face. Reflexively, he rolled over upon his back. I raised the brick above my head again, felt a sense of delirium engulfing my body, began laughing, became happy, wanted to kill him, needed perhaps to kill him . . . the tears continued to roll down the sides of my face, and I continued to laugh, to cry, to scream . . .

I was crying and screaming still when someone grabbed my arm in midair, wrestling me to the floor—two, three, how many? I was crying and screaming too when the ambulance came for Walter, crying and screaming still when my mother, lecturing me all the way, led me from the police station. I did not stop until sometime the next morning, when, exhausted, I fell asleep.

But the next day, when my mother told me that Walter would not die, I began to cry again. She believed, I think, that these were tears of remorse, of repentance. I managed a smile, thought of how little this woman knew about her son, wanted to take her face in my hands, look into her tired eyes, move my lips close to her ears, say, "Momma, I'm crying because he didn't die. I wish I had killed him. I'm sorry that I did not." But I said nothing, dressed, took my notebook, and went to the garden, sat and wrote and fantasized. Because my book had not been a success, I thought, did not mean that I had to stop writing; indeed, I knew that I could not. I knew, deep down, beyond the anger and rage, that Walter was not the real enemy, only the symbol, and that the weapons I had used against him I could not use against them. But I could use those weapons I had polished and garnished, largely because of my father, to right all the wrongs done to me, to avenge myself, in isolation, in seclusion, could use them also to rewrite the past, to make it less fuzzy and more visible.

No, I would never have the powerful voice of my father, never be able to use words the way he did; but I could use them in another way, in a way that he could not. Perhaps, in so doing, I could end the hostility between us, the antagonism, tell him that I knew why this is so, that I am older now, that I meant nothing by the words I uttered when I was not so old, that I did not mean them.

The things that I realize now, from a distance of so many years, I am certain that I knew then. At least I knew my own feelings, if not those of others—though I could speculate about others—and during the course of the past, I am not so sure that I was not right in my speculation concerning my father. I remember a time when he would hold me, pull me toward him, bouncing me up and down on his knee. I was not frightened of him then, because he seemed affectionate, warm. I remember too when he seemed to stop being all those things, when he seemed to change abruptly, almost overnight, to becoming cold, distant, calculating.

He had finished a lecture, on the makeshift stand in the vacant lot of the poolroom. Accepting the applause, he hoisted me atop his shoulder, and announced to the crowd: "This is my boy, here, Addison, Jr. My boy." The crowd had responded again with applause and cheers. Bewildered and bashful, I had leaned my face close to his, feeling the hairs on the side of his face, asked, "Daddy, why you tellin them people I'm your boy?" He had held me back from him at arm's length, his eyes no longer on the people now beginning to disperse, and said, hurt and anger in his eyes, "What's the matter? Don't you want people to know you my son?"

I knew that he was hurt, but I did not know what to say, wanted to say something, to ingratiate myself, to stop his hurt; I said nothing, began to cry. He led me away after the meeting, did not buy me an ice cream cone as usual, did not try to gain my favors as usual, at the expense of my mother. In the following days, he said very little to me, seemed to be trying to push me closer and closer toward my mother. Once when I came near, he had pushed me away, saying, "You're not my boy; you're your mother's boy, aren't you?" With my mother sitting on the other side of the room, staring at me, he, sitting distant on the other side, staring too. I had stood looking from one to the other, head down, confused, bewildered. A few days later, when he and my mother were scrambling, wrestling over his wallet, the wallet fell to the floor and I picked it up. Both began to admonish me to bring them the wallet and I stood in the middle of the floor again, looking from one to the other, staring first here, then there, being pulled by one voice, pulled back by another, until, in total confusion, I threw the wallet in the direction of my mother, ran crying from the room. The next day my mother and I moved into a new house.

I wanted to tell him that I remembered those events, those days and others, that I was sorry for them, that I was, however, too little to be able to make choices, I could not decide between him and my mother, but I loved them both. I wanted to tell him, also, that though I admired him, I was angry with him too for forcing me to make such choices. I was enraged against him for deserting me, not protecting me as Alice's father protected her and her brother, but leaving me alone, defenseless—as I had then believed. As I grew older and sat in his living room, time after time, feeling terrified, cowering before him, and resentful, I wanted to tell him that he seemed more concerned with ideas than with his own son, more concerned with saving other people than he was with saving me, and that sometimes I hated him for this. But I also wanted to tell him that this hatred was not real, was only momentary, and that he could erase it forever, if he would only take me in his arms, hold me as before, ask me again if I was not proud to be his son. I could never tell him any of this verbally, but I could write it, putting it down on paper for him to read. By the time I had decided that I would do this, trying as best I could to explain what I knew and what I felt, he was dead —struck down by a massive hemorrhage of the brain.

CHAPTER 4

My father died in 1952, two years after my graduation from high school and a short stint in the Air Force. I saw him seldom during the final years of his life and on those few occasions when we did meet, our relations were more distant, more strained. This was attributable not so much to him as to me, for I had begun to suffer from a profound sense of despair, in which I withdrew, much more frequently and for longer durations of time than previously, from unnecessary contact. I isolated myself from those about me. During those years, when I was moving into my twenties, the despair was precipitated, I suppose, by the shallow victory I had won by graduating from high school.

The tension began to set in on the morning after graduation, after having marched the night before (as I had so often imagined) in black gown and cap to the tune of "Pomp and Circumstance." My old antagonists from Huntington High School were not there, being busy with their own commencement exercises, but they knew that I was graduating, that I had, indeed, endured that last year. In addition, my classmates had given me a pen and a notebook, with the inscription that I was to continue writing, that they expected great things of me.

Once the ceremonies were over, however, once the congratulations from family and well-wishers were delivered, I began to reflect upon the meaning of having graduated from high school. I realized that it had meant really very little. Finally, I was on my own, alone, able now to call upon no support, not even that which came from the antagonism of enemies or even the closeness of classmates. Outside of my father, there was no one in the town with whom I held a close relationship, no one with whom I might seek comradeship. I could no longer enjoy the hostility of teachers, the enmity of fellow students. A high school graduate with no means of entering college, I would no longer be tolerated in the homes of the mulattoes and, outside of accomplishing something spectacular, I would never be able to approach their status, secure their recognition. The circumstances of my family dictated that I take my mother's advice and find a job in the shipyard. Such prospects only added to my discomfort. The result of this state of affairs was that I developed hypochondria—imagined myself afflicted by the most dreadful diseases. I also began to drink regularly, and ended up in the United States Air Force.

Though my tenure in the Air Force was short-lived—I was discovered to have a heart condition, some six months after enlistment—I gained valuable experience which was to serve me well in the coming years. Thrown together with men from all backgrounds, ages, and experiences, I learned much about the needs, desperations, and pains of other men, and much more about my own. From a white recruit, not much older than myself, I learned something about the dimension of the American race problem that my isolation from whites in Virginia had prevented my knowing heretofore.

Donald was from Tennessee, blond, thick-muscled, short in stature. We had been thrown together on a work detail, and quickly became friends. We talked about mutual problems, concerns, though I told him little and he told me a great deal. Soon we began to meet more frequently during the course of basic training, in the mess hall and the PX. I learned that he had joined the Air Force after having brutally assaulted his wife, whom he had caught in bed with another man, that he was planning on making a career out of the service; that he was fond of his Tennessee. It was this fondness for his hometown which caused him, I believe, to ask me to accompany him home during furlough time. I could not discern, then, the conflict that developed within him following his offer, and thought little at that time of the enthusiasm with which the offer had been made, and the ensuing panic, once he realized that the offer struck home.

"Gayle," he had said after describing his hometown, "man they got some good-looking women out there . . . Oh, man! . . . Look, when we get a furlough—we get it about the same time—you got to come home with me . . . I mean it . . . I can put you up . . ."

There were five of us at the table, two Blacks and three whites, and the silence suddenly became gravelike. Noting the abrupt silence, Donald looked from face to face, shook his head sadly, closed and finally opened his eyes, pounding his first into his hand: "I don't give a damn about the segregation, Gayle, I don't . . ."

It was evident, however, that he did. In his enthusiasm, he had forgotten an important fact about his country. Being in the Air Force, where one was first defined as airman, he had almost lost sight of the demarcation line—color—color, which separated one man from another. I knew he was distressed about a state of affairs over which he had no control, but we both knew that neither he nor I would challenge the southern mores, that I would not go home with him, nor he with me, that our friendship would survive only so long as we remained within the perimeters of the air base.

I had felt a tenseness, an uneasiness then, feeling sorry for Donald and the conflict he was undergoing, but I had had no cognizance of the trap into which he had been placed by his history. I thought then that my father, after all, had been right. Segregation had managed to afflict victim and victimizer alike. There were those Donalds of the world, who had been shuttled into patterns not of their own making, and who became, at times, distressed as a result of them.

Our friendship deteriorated after that evening. Donald was never able to talk to me without a sense of guilt and outrage darkening his face, without becoming apologetic or condescending. I felt unable to sit with him without feeling uncomfortable, strange, unwanted. The friendship finally dissolved into nothing more than exchanged greetings and polite conversation. He had, I supposed, discovered something about himself which he had not known, could not comprehend, and he was, I think, both angry and frightened.

But I was to discover something about myself, equally frightening. Sitting in the town one night with three friends, Clift, Reginald, and Clarence, in Geneva, New York, where the base was situated, I had been drinking beer at a local bar. A tall, well-shaped white woman with blond, shoulder-length hair had sat nearby drinking vodka, one drink following the next. We had watched the frequency with which she drank, commented on the quantity she consumed, and took further notice of her departure, as she staggered from the table toward the door. Clift rose up instantaneously, and the rest of us followed. The woman staggered down the street, off the main avenue onto side streets of dimly lit two-family homes, darkened by trees and shrubbery. We four Black men had followed in hot, though casual pursuit.

There was an ominous silence about the way we walked/stalked. Though there had been no conversation between us, we knew that the word "rape" was foremost in our minds, knew that we were tracking our prey to some isolated area. Once we had her there, we knew that each of us in turn would assault her. I was conscious of the rapid beating of my own heart, of the tension in my temples, the tightening of my muscles, the fear and the pity mingled with a single obsession. Once or twice I thought of the girl—the cruelty of the coming act, the simple fact of violating another human being. I thought too of the consequences, jail, perhaps even death, but certainly dishonor, and I am sure the others entertained similar thoughts. But we were driven by an obsession that I cannot now understand, locked together in a drama, in which no roles had been prepared, no lines prescribed. We felt carried away by the immediacy of the moment, not so much because of lust—sex was very easy to come by in Geneva—but because of something akin to a need for power, for dominance, for release of outraged, pent-up emotions. When the woman disappeared into one of the two-family houses—split seconds before she would have entered into a grassy, isolated area, we stopped. Each breathing hard, we looked at one another, shaking our heads. Relieved, we walked back in silence to the main street.

Two days later, when I jotted down the details of the incident in my notebook, I was ashamed at what I had discovered about myself, unable to discern what blind obsession had led me to engage in the stalking of a drunken woman. I realized that all my rational instincts had been momentarily paralyzed, that I had ceased to think and reflect upon the consequences of my actions. Contrary to everything that I had learned from my father, I had been passionately caught up in the act itself, overwhelmed by it, controlled by it. This realization intensified my discomfort, drove me, even here among so many men, into isolation, with my typewriter and my books.

Discharged from the Air Force before my enlistment time was up, I returned to Newport News, bringing hundreds of pages of typewritten notes, including work on a novel, several short stories, and poetry. I also carried home memories of tenuous, easily forgotten relationships, along with an honorable discharge and a passport which would get me out of the country. I had no intention of remaining in Newport News beyond spending the last of the mustering-out pay I had received, but I had no idea of where I would go or what I would do once I found somewhere to go. While in the Air Force, I had been submitting short stories and poems to magazines—I had found names, addresses, and sales pitches in writer's magazines—and had accumulated some six or seven rejection slips in all. Once back in Newport News (and declared a failure once again, since I could not even stay four years in the Air Force), I wrote with abandon and nervous energy, amassing still more rejection slips to show for it. To dull the echoes of the remarks made about "Miss Carrie's boy," I turned to alcohol and women. Both left me feeling more distraught and sent me back to the isolation of the typewriter. I consciously remained away from my father, visiting him only once in the year following my return, motivated by a new sense of guilt. On making out allowances for parents upon entering the Air Force, I had made out one for my mother, refusing to do the same for my father.

I knew he would have known nothing about this, but I was unaware of why I had done it, especially since I now looked upon him with different eyes, wanting somehow to reveal what I had remembered. Looking back from this vantage point after my bouts with Raphael, my analyst, from the age of forty-two, I wonder if I were not saying through actions that what happened to us that day on the platform, you and I, when I questioned my being an extension of you—your son—I wonder if I were not saying then that I did not want to belong to you, no, not to you or to anyone, that I wanted to keep all of me, for myself, wanted to be a reflection of no one, and that somehow the great contradiction of my life was that I had wanted to belong to someone, that I was, perhaps, a reflection of many images in many mirrors.

The guilt mingled with rage, contempt, anger, remorse, became secondary when he died, some two days before a friend discovered him, alone, in the two-room flat he occupied near the city limits of Hampton. I greeted the announcement of his death matter-of-factly, from a drunken stupor, and managed to pull myself together only when his sisters and brothers came from Philadelphia and Baltimore to bury him. I sat dry-eyed in the funeral home, looking at the stranger before me, done up in wax, eyes closed, lips stilled. Waves of something like remorse engulfed me as I sat in the front row of the church listening to the minister sermonizing about the man who had had only contempt for ministers and their sermons. Though reliving some of our happier moments, even some of our debates, I was still unable to bring myself to cry. The fact that he was gone had not yet, would not for many years, really permeate my mind. The fact of my loneliness and isolation was as pronounced as when he had been alive. I remember remaining at the freshly dug grave in Gloucester long after the others had gone, in this cemetery where my grandparents and aunts had been buried before him. I didn't think so much about my father or his passing (though I did not, for some reason, want to leave the cemetery) but of my aunt, a woman with an aristocratic nose and sharp penetrating eyes. She had stood beside me during the viewing of the casket, dignified and regal as once he had been, dabbing her eyes meticulously with a white handkerchief.

Earlier, during a previous conversation, her strong, tender touch on my arm, she had said, "Now, Junior, don't you stay in this place. I used to tell your daddy . . . come on up North . . . at least a smart Black man got a chance up there . . . But he wouldn't come. But you come . . . don't you stay here . . ."

I did not realize it then, but I thought of her words there, in that cemetery, because I had understood the pointlessness of staying in Virginia. It was now an appropriate time to leave, to take my typewriter, my notes, and my rejection slips and go forward, to what I did not know, but certainly something important. Not only would I settle/equal the score between myself and my adversaries, I would also make everything right by my father. Twenty-one years old, sitting before my father's grave, as the cars passed noisily on the road outside the cemetery, I could not have understood why I thought not of my father and our relationship, but of revenge and of the need to prove myself.

I did not accept my aunt's offer to visit Philadelphia until some two years later, having arrived there via Newark, New Jersey, and Detroit, Michigan. One week after my father died, I left home headed for Newark, where Benny, an old acquaintance, now lived. I preferred being completely on my own, not obligated to relatives.

Benny, slightly older than I, was a dark brown, handsome young man, with a boyish smile framed in a boyish face. Because he was not mulatto, our association in high school had not been strong—though we had been close acquaintances. On one of his return visits to Newport News, he had invited me to Newark, assuring me that I could rent a room at his rooming house. Shortly after I arrived, I discovered that he was not the Benny I had known in high school. He had become somewhat angrier, more cynical, less trusting.

The Benny of Huntington High School had been well liked. Outgoing, confident, courageous, he had sported a scar, the result of sacrificing himself so that his friends could escape from a gang of bullies. There had been other scars, I found out, much more severe and permanent than the one inflicted by the local gang. Shortly after leaving Newport News, Benny had married, become a father, and, with the hope of buying a home, had begun to work two jobs in South Orange, New Jersey. Benny had been jolted, almost crushed when, arriving home unexpectedly one day, he had discovered another man in bed with his wife. In time, he was able to forgive her—even to hold himself responsible. Although she never brought a man to his bed again, Benny gradually came to accept the fact that she had not given them up either. Separation followed a brutal court fight for possession of the child, who was awarded to the mother. It had left him bitter and mistrustful, a man seeking vengeance.

Women became his enemies, good for providing bed and money, nether-world creatures whom one treated roughly, never completely trusting. Women had become transformed into bitches, scavengers, devourers of masculinity. Cruelly, Ben played Black and white women against one another. From each of his victimized conquests he extracted photos and once he had seduced a Black newcomer, for example, he would produce the

photo of her white contemporary and vice versa, pointing out in
descriptive terms the superiority of the rival in the act of lovemaking.

Toward men, however, Ben showed the loyalty of old, believing, I suspect, that we were all bound up in the common fight
against a similar antagonist. Due to his help, I was able to rent a
room, and four days later to find a job as an orderly at the
Bethlehem Hospital. In what was to be a long succession of jobs
as an orderly, this first was my most difficult. Despite the fact that
we were allowed to take temperatures and to read pulses, a job as-
sociated with interns, we were usually bedpan carriers, func-
tionaries, the lackeys of the hospital staff. We were addressed as
Mr. and Mrs./Miss, but to me such addresses did nothing to
lessen the degradation I felt from the job itself. Unable to stem
the old despair, never completely dissipated, I found myself once
again acting condescending roles, reliving fantasies. To whatever
nurses and interns would listen, I broadcast the fact that I was
writing a novel, talking of books and writers. By so doing, I hoped
to appear as other than an orderly, an emptier of bedpans. I went
out of my way to talk to the two mulatto interns on the predominantly white staff, tried ingratiating myself with the mulatto
nurses, imagined dating both them and the white nurses. At
night, I worked continually on a new novel, dreaming the dreams
of old. I distanced myself, I imagined, from my Black fellow
workers by my ability to speak well, to write creatively, to feign
the mannerisms of the hospital's professional class.

That there was no distance between myself and the other Black
orderlies was demonstrated by a patient, dying from cancer of the
brain. Mrs. Martin, a tall skinny white woman with stringy hair
and a long face, occupied a private room on the fifth ward. A patient for only four weeks, she had, in that time, been reduced almost to a skeleton. The terminal ailment had transformed her
into something of a living zombie, who, during moments of consciousness, could be heard screaming up and down the ward. On
this particular day, when she was being ministered to by a nurse
and intern, the intern thumbing through the chart at the foot of
her bed, the nurse dispensing medication, I had entered the room
to empty her bedpan. Inside the door, moving toward the bed, I
was halted by her outburst. It was as if my very presence had
given her renewed life, galvanized her into action. "What is that
dirty nigger doing in here?" she asked, voice shrill, high-pitched.

The intern looked embarrassed, the nurse, quizzical; both avoided my eyes. Mrs. Martin's voice rose, shriller, more panic-filled. ". . . that dirty nigger . . . quick . . . quick . . . cover me . . ."—pause—". . . am I covered?" The intern, avoiding my eyes, turned to her, soothingly. "He won't hurt you. He's a nice colored boy." Turning toward me, he winked. I stood frozen, wanted to go out of the door, wanted to move toward the bedpan.

Mrs. Martin looked fearfully around the intern, at me, then appealed to him again: "Don't let him rape me; please don't let that dirty nigger rape me." The intern motioned for me to leave. As I closed the door, he was reassuring her again, "That's all right, Mrs. Martin, he's gone . . . he won't hurt you, now, see . . . ?"

Angrily I stalked down the hall, thinking that I should have said something, should have defended myself, should have maybe slammed the door when she first began to scream. My anger and animosity were directed, I know now, not so much against Mrs. Martin for humiliating me, but instead because she had not distinguished me from other orderlies, other Negroes, despite the fact that I had always been polite, well-mannered, well-spoken. And if she, brain tumor and all, near death, were able to see through my masquerade, then surely the others were able to do so too, were able to understand that I was nothing more than an orderly, an emptier of bedpans. What did it matter that I enunciated my words more clearly and correctly than other Blacks, that I took two baths a day, that I used deodorant unsparingly, that I avoided slang, spoke softly, walked correctly, that I read books and wrote poetry and novels? It mattered little to the Mrs. Martins and to those like her, no, no more so than what I really thought myself to be had mattered to the people in Virginia. Like them, Mrs. Martin had been able to telescope beneath the camouflage, to reveal the man hiding within.

Wanting to strike out at something, to unleash my anger, I stormed through the eye, ear, and nose clinic, bypassing the outstretched hands of fellow workers, brushing past them hurriedly. I was almost through the clinic, had moved beyond the patients lounging on folding chairs, standing in line, was moving so fast and so furiously that I did not see the woman crossing directly in front of me, leading a little boy by the hand. "Why the hell don't you watch where you going?" I asked at the point of collision.

She recovered, scowled at me through dark, hostile eyes, threw out a hip to meet her descending hand: "Why in the hell don't you watch where you going, *mister*." The boy at her side, who had been untouched in the collision, looked from me to her, amused.

"Look," I barked, "there's a whole aisle over there, see . . . ?"

She ignored my outstretched hand, said, "Since you know where it is, why don't you use it?"

Something in her manner, the tone of her voice, salty, daring, combative, forced me to halt, cool down. I noticed her breasts for the first time, rounded large, looked down at her legs, shapely, attractive, retreated: "Look, I'm not wrong, but I apologize, anyway."

She laughed at the accent I had shifted to now that the anger had been abated, the one I used to impress the interns and nurses: "Why you talkin like that, now?"

I threw up my hands in disgust, shouted over my shoulder, "You're stupid." And bounded away.

One week later I returned to the clinic to search for her and, finding her, walked over to where she stood in line. "How am I talking today?" I asked.

"I don't know," she said. "Say something."

"My name is Addison," I replied. "When you finish, let's have some coffee."

She laughed, a blush coming to her light tan cheeks. "You still talk funny. But my name is Yvonne. I got something to do today."

"How about tomorrow?"

"Tomorrow, I work."

"When, then?"

"I don't know! I come back to the clinic, next week."

I said, "Okay, when I get off . . . three o'clock." I looked again at her breasts, her legs; the boy stared, watching the movement of my eyes. I patted him on the head and walked off.

Her legs and breasts were her most attractive features, dwarfing her well-rounded face, the short, boyish-cut hair, the bold, daring brown eyes. Tanned, sunburnt skin, prevented her from being a mulatto, but the smooth evenness of the brown color moved her also out of the category of Blacks such as myself. I was to discover much about her in the coming weeks, was to be drawn, as if by an overpowering magnet, not so much to her, but to what I learned. The tremendous ability, springing free now to empathize with women, to suffer with them, obscured almost totally my inability to distinguish real emotions from those feigned.

Yvonne's history was part of a legend, painted so often for me in bold, stark, garish colors by the madonna that once she began to relate it, I became hooked, longing to hear more, to be able to empathize more, to suffer more. She had separated from her husband, a brutal man who used her as the object of his own frustrations. "Soons he get his pay check," she related, "he stops off somewhere and spends it. Then he come home and starts a fight, because he don't have any money." Besides the mental wounds, there were physical ones: at the base of her spine, where he had struck her with a sugar bowl; a large gash at the mouth of her vagina, which had taken three stitches to heal—the result of teeth tearing against skin. These and other such acts had led her to take her son, Jamie, and move into an apartment with her mother and two sisters.

Surfacing in my consciousness were memories of Mr. Walter, along with other such men whom the madonna had known. I never questioned the authenticity of such stories, would never be able to regard the bearer as anything but a victim.

I hated Yvonne's husband, thought I did not know him, and instinctively, impulsively, I wanted to help her, to right the wrongs done to her. I discerned an eternal sadness in her eyes which I wanted to erase, a dimmed light I wanted to bring back to life. I wanted to rescue her from misery, past and present, to protect her from evils yet unknown. In time, this obsession would outweigh all other attractions, even the physical, would transform her from woman to martyr, would cause me to fall in love not so much with the real person, but with the idea.

How could I have known then that Yvonne wanted not a savior, but a lover? Having projected my own needs upon her, I became oblivious to what hers really were, indeed, lost sight of the fact that she had any. I treated her with pity as one might treat a sad, defeated mother, became overbearingly affectionate. Though I embraced her seldom, and never without feelings of guilt, I was abnormally protective, constantly I invented scenarios in which I became a writer, wrote a best-selling novel, rescuing her from sadness and drudgery. That I was robbing her of her individuality, stifling her, binding her to me, she knew better than I. When she finally discovered a rationale for breaking the affair—I had lied to her about my age—she did so quickly, decisively, and I plunged headlong into a period of severe depression.

I was not to know such depression again, until twenty years later, when other events would send me close to mental breakdown. Always before, even in the period when I felt unbelievably overwhelmed, there were the dreams and fantasies which kept me going—I could manage, after a while, to move to my typewriter, to unburden myself in badly written prose. Now, however, I was immobilized, unable and unwilling to think beyond the present situation, forbidding my mind from moving into other, safer areas. There was first the doubt, the inability of the savior to believe that he had been rejected. For how could she reject me, knowing what would happen to her? She would go back to meet men like her husband, those who would abuse her, bring her pain. I pictured her lying awake, night after night, clutching Jamie in her arms, cowering before some man who terrorized them both. How could she leave me, the barrier to all of that?

After the doubt, came a brief period of hope that things could be set right by a face-to-face confrontation. I took the lonely bus ride to her house, some three miles away in darkest Newark, where the decaying buildings stood like faded gargoyles. Bribing a teen-ager to call Yvonne's home, I ascertained that she was not in, and took up vigilance outside. I sat on the stoop, walked from corner to corner, continuously scanning the area: the garbage piled high, the faces of the people expressing suspicion, curiosity. At three o'clock in the morning, Yvonne finally stepped out of a late model Buick, a coal-black man behind the wheel. She reached over, kissed him. I froze; I turned my head, wanted to walk away, feeling guilty and ashamed for spying on her. As she stepped on the stoop, I appeared in the shadow of one of the gargoyles, called her name. The anguish and desperation in my voice caused her to halt, pause: "Addison, what are you doing here? I meant what I said."

"Yvonne," I begged, "let's talk."

The gargoyles were grinning, mocking. "There ain't nothing to talk about." There were tears in her eyes, a strain in her voice. She placed a hand on my shoulder, then abruptly drew it away, regained her composure: "Look, I got to go to work in the morning."

I followed her up the stairs, pleading, cajoling. She reached the door of her apartment, fumbled nervously with the lock, flung open her door, looked piteously upon me, and closed it. I stood for a while, tears in my eyes, watching the closed door, before finally walking back to be one with the gargoyles.

I walked slowly, unsteadily, like a drunken man, weaving and twisting my way past other gargoyles, downtown where the neon lights were, where the pimps and whores plied their trade. Once again, I felt victimized, conspired against. Devoid of all strength to continue the struggle, willing to admit to enemies real and imagined, "This is the end, you have won, I am done." I ended up in the vestibule of a Catholic church, not noticing the heavy-set priest who eyed me suspiciously, scowling at my casual attire. Whatever tears were still visible, were in the form of streaks, invisible stains on my dark skin. The priest halted me just inside the vestibule, blocked my path, nervously questioned me. He thought I had come to rob him.

"I want to pray," I said, from some fog deep within.

"Are you Catholic?" he asked, still nervous, still unsure.

"No! I don't believe in God."

His eyebrows arched, causing the lines to tighten in his face; his mouth opened in surprise, but no words came. Finally, he stretched out his hands, palms opened wide. "But then why come here?"

"Why not?" I asked.

He shrugged his shoulders. Moved aside. His eyes followed me to a row of seats near the back, watched as I entered the row and fell to my knees. I had not come to this place to pray, to call upon the God of my mother for salvation; I had come, instead, to dramatize my situation for myself, to wallow in my own self-pity (did I enjoy this drama, then unfolding?), to align myself with the metaphor of all human suffering. The tears began to come again, the convulsions to wrack my body. I conjured up visions of Yvonne. She had followed me to the church, saw me prostrate, saw the death wish in my eyes, remained unmoved. "Why," I asked through my tears, throwing my question to a phantom, a mental creation, "can't you see how much I suffer? Why can't you understand how close I am to taking my own life? Come, Yvonne, come, come closer, look into my eyes, see my suffering, these are the eyes of a dead man."

I do not know when the daylight came, when I left the church, sidled past another priest. I remember being back at the rooming house, bottles of wine in my hands, remember that Benny and Scotty, another roommate, were preparing to go to work, that I brushed past them, ran hurriedly to my room. I began to drink, hoping to become drunk quickly, wanted to stop seeing phantoms, and to become incoherent. I remember, too, vaguely, drinking one bottle of wine after another, becoming sick, drifting off into sweet delirium. I remember Benny's knock on the door—he wanted to borrow a sports coat for the evening—remember that I was hung over, but that he did not comment upon my condition.

The wine had not helped alleviate the pain. Yvonne, phantom-like, still moved misty-like before my eyes. I remember looking into the mirror, commenting upon my ugliness, feeling my ugliness, rummaging around in my brain for evidence of a time when I had not been ugly. Had there ever been such a time? I concluded that the oracles of old had been correct all along, that those who had designated me a failure, destined to a violent end, had been right all along. My very existence seemed an affront, an abomination. I remember picking up the razor from the dresser top, extracting a blade, and making a slight incision in the vein on my left arm. I remember crying uncontrollably as the blood began to trickle slowly, thinking of how guilty everyone would feel once they discovered that I had been driven to take my own life.

I do not, however, remember screaming, do not remember when the ambulance came. When I woke up in the hospital Benny and Scotty were there. They said something to me before I drifted off into sleep. When I awoke again, they were still there. The doctors did not believe Benny and Scotty's story that I had cut myself accidentally. But after a few days, during which I was kept under observation and questioned by psychiatrists, I was allowed to leave. Three days after my release, Scotty informed me, "We called Yvonne that night, man, but she wouldn't come. She through, baby. But what you gonna kill yourself for? It ain't gonna bring her back. It ain't gonna do no good. Ain't no woman worth that. You gonna forget her anyway . . . in a few months, you gonna forget her."

How could I explain to either him or Benny, who echoed his thoughts, what I did not then know myself? It was not because of Yvonne that I had come close to taking my life. No, there were ephemeral ghosts of the past, to a large degree of my own making

—figments of my own psyche—which, having grown as I grew, matured as I matured, were capable now of moving me from simple states of despair to more extreme ones. Killing myself was merely another way of striking back at my enemies, of making people notice me, accept me.

I did know then, however, after weeks of thinking and isolating myself once again, that Yvonne was not the mechanism, was only an insignificant part of the cause. For it was not so much Yvonne as woman that I had loved but Yvonne as an idea, Yvonne divested of all corporeal being, truly a phantom of the mind, and one which I could not lightly surrender. I knew, therefore, that I could remain in Newark no longer, that depression would cause me to cling to the idea, that the idea itself was so imprinted upon my psyche that I would embellish it still further, make her appear less woman, less human. I knew I would see her face in the gargoyles, feel her presence in the parks, imagine her near as I walked the silent streets. She would be there in every part of that city where we had gone before, her laughter and Jamie's would reach out to me from every bus. The scent of her would invade my nostrils, cutting through the city's pollution, wherever I went. No, I could surrender the woman, but never the idea of the woman until I had removed myself. Thus, three weeks after having attempted to take my life, with my metal suitcase, typewriter, and notebooks in hand, I boarded a bus to Detroit.

The three-day ride put a distance between myself and Yvonne the woman. The time and distance, however, only magnified Yvonne the idea. Once, like a child, I would have been captivated as towns, cities, and their magnificent sights rolled by before my eyes; once I would have wanted to write a poem after seeing many beautiful sunsets and sunrises. At one time, I would have been jolted back into melancholia while watching trees—giant evergreens, skinny birches—recede in the distance as the bus pushed onward. Happier times would have been evoked, like the memory of my father and mother driving to Gloucester, Virginia, with me sitting in the back of the car, watching other trees disappear into the distance.

I saw very little and I slept very little during this trip. I thought about Yvonne, reminisced about the good times, lacerating myself. The same fantasies emerged as previously, conjuring up mental scenes of self-masochism, of self-prostration. The army veteran

returning home to Detroit whom I met on the bus, talked much
and told a storehouse of ribald jokes, seemingly unaware that my
answers to his questions and my laughter at his jokes were forced,
mechanical.

Near the end of the trip, something of the old optimism returned—and I began to compose new scenarios. My absence from
Yvonne would cause a hunger in her breast, would convince her
that she needed me, would force her to want to take me back. I
would get a job in Detroit, find an apartment, furnish it well and
send for her and Jamie. With Newark behind us, as though it had
never happened, we might begin again . . .

I arrived in Detroit on a warm September morning, feeling better about myself, the world. The veteran helped me secure a small
room on the corner of John R. and Brush Street, which was, I discovered soon enough, the red-light district. Houses of prostitution
lined the blocks, sharing occupancy with bars and restaurants.
The streets were loud with the noise of the living—blaring, shrieking music, laughing, playing children, the seductive come-ons of
the prostitutes. A white prostitute offered herself to me for two
dollars. I turned her down. I also turned down an offer to buy a
watch from a ten-year-old boy. I paused to witness a floating crap
game, wanted to join, but was afraid to risk my remaining
seventy-five dollars. Later that night, I bought a bottle of cheap
wine and drank myself into a numbless sleep, seeing still the
phantom, the abstraction, the idea: Yvonne.

I awoke suddenly, some three hours later, drenched in sweat,
my mind dulled. I had an obsession to call Yvonne, a panic to
talk to her, to lay out my plans. Dressing hurriedly, I moved back
into the desperate streets, which had changed only slightly from
the daylight hours. Weaving in and out of the small crowd of
prostitutes and customers, I found a telephone at the far end of a
noisy bar and dialed her number. She was not home. My hands
began to shake, sweat, my obsession intensified; now, I had to talk
to her. I called at twenty-minute intervals, slamming the phone
down violently when the person-to-person operator informed me
that she was not in. I ordered drink after drink until about four
o'clock in the morning, when her irritated voice sounded over the
telephone. She said she hoped that I was fine, she wished me luck,
was glad that I had left Newark, thought that this was the best
for both of us, thanked me for calling, asked me not to call again,

and hung up. She had monopolized the conversation, hearing little of what I had to say about my plans. Staring at the lifeless telephone, I grew angrier and more surprised. Stifling the growing rage, I stopped the tears beginning to form in my eyes, stilled my shaking body, walked out of the bar and headed down Brush Street. I found the white prostitute, made a deal with her, picked up another bottle of wine. For ten dollars, she stayed with me until noon of the next day.

I remained in Detroit for only five days before leaving for Philadelphia. The city was in the middle of an auto strike and jobs were difficult to come by. I knew that I could not return to Newark, nor could I return home to Newport News. Both places represented monuments to my abysmal worthlessness, testaments to my failure as a human being. I had meanwhile whittled my original seventy-five dollars down to fifteen, and the prospects of adding to that sum seemed negligible. Once again, I boarded the Greyhound bus, this time for a destination which, I hoped, would offer more positive rewards.

I was welcomed into the household of my aunt by my uncle James, my cousin Elizabeth, who was older than I, and my aunt herself. I occupied the room next to my cousin, a beautiful woman, tall and Black, regal like her mother, with long shapely legs, protruding breasts. Throughout my three-week stay, Elizabeth would appeal to me to go to church with her; she would never know that I wanted to go to bed with her instead.

Three days after arriving in Philadelphia, I found a job as an orderly at the University of Pennsylvania hospital. Like the nurse's aides and orderlies at Bethlehem Hospital, most were Black. There were a small number of Black nurses, and three Black interns, all mulatto. I began, though with less vigor than before, to patronize the mulattoes, became obsequious in their presence. They ignored me, answered my queries with short, quick answers, did not tarry long in conversation with me.

I had no such difficulty establishing a relationship with the other orderlies, however. Charles, a lanky, brown man, wore his hair in a marcel—straightened, plastered down to his skull. He and Bubber, another orderly, wasted no time trying to convince me of the positive rewards to be gained from wearing a marcel. "Dig this," Charles would say on more than one occasion when a number of us sat out the lunch hour in the locker room—running his fingers through his hair, "not a nap here . . . not *a* nap, brother!" He would turn from me to Bubber, who sported a *quo vadis*, for support.

"Look, Gayle," Bubber would come in on cue, "my hair used to be worse than yours, man. Yeah, I mean it, nappy right up to the edges, damn near killed me every time I tried to comb the motherfucker . . . I got that shit cut off and, now . . . dig this!" He would stand, pull a comb from his back pocket, move it effortlessly through his hair. He would hand me the comb, implore me to duplicate his feat. I did not have to try. I knew that the comb would not run easily through my hair, knew that my hair was nappy—unmanageable—that no matter what I did to it in the morning, in the afternoon it would be curled, rolled into balls, offensive.

I knew something, however, about the legend of the marcel, which had been famous in the ghettos of Newark. It was a more sophisticated term for "conking" or straightening one's hair. Once a week the wearer of the marcel went to a barbershop specializing in the process, allowed his hair to be drenched in a lye-like mixture until it was, literally, plastered to his scalp. He then sat for forty minutes under a hair dryer before having the plastered hair waved and formed into patterns by expert fingers. Marcels came in two styles, the straight marcel, requiring a longer length of hair than usual, and the *quo vadis*, cut short and smoothed down so that strands of hair fell across the forehead.

The marcel, I know now, was an incredible invention for those like myself who were ashamed of their physical features, who lacked self-esteem, who somewhere in their background, had their visions of Alexanders and fathers of mulatto girlfriends. It was a miracle bequeathed to the poor and black—few mulattoes needed or obtained marcels—an instrument of transformation better than any religion, because it called for the minimum of sacrifice, while offering the maximum of reward. Possession of a marcel brought immediate status and recognition to the wearer, made him overnight one with entertainers and hustlers, made him more attractive to women. Even white people acted differently toward the marcel wearer, found him more attractive, one supposes, in an exotic sense. Those who did not laugh at the spectacle looked upon him as a Negro outside the norm, more likely to be less docile and subservient than his brother.

Yet the marcel was—and each wearer knew this—an imitation, a substitute for the real thing, which took money and time to maintain. He did not know, however, that the status it afforded on the one hand, it snatched back on the other, for the wearer, if not an entertainer, was immediately identifiable as lower class, a Black of darker complexion. Measured against the real thing—the wavy hair of the mulattoes or the naturally straight hair of whites —it was gimmicky, unreal, unnatural.

I might then have realized all these things had I been more steady of mind, had I wanted to think rationally. The truth is that I did not. The idea of Yvonne, though receding, remained still, and my typewriter lay, along with my half-finished novel, untouched since my flight from Newark. Looking, perhaps, for support to bolster my own low opinion of myself, I had ventured, frequently, into the past, going back to the earliest days, always the saddest, most depressing ones. Alexander and Doretha appeared, now, finally identified as the major metaphors of my life—those whose examples, were I to be saved from enemies, protected, allowed to do great things, I need, no, must emulate. How different things might have been for me, I told myself, had I been mulatto, had Alexander's or Alice's father been my own. How much better the world and my place in it might have been had I been born mulatto—with light skin, small lips, good hair.

Yes, by becoming a writer, someone whom the white people would notice and recognize, I would be forgiven ugliness. I could compensate for my lack of fine physical features, my dark skin would be welcomed, even among the mulattoes. But in my continuing state of despondency, I had concluded that I was earmarked for failure, that I would never emulate Richard Wright, that I would accumulate one rejection slip after another, constantly reminded of my own failure. Why not, then, the marcel, why not this partial victory over my ugliness? Why not move closer, even in fantasy tinged with some reality, to the Alexander of my childhood longings, to the interns of my adult ones?

Two weeks after moving out of my aunt's house into an apartment of my own, I had my hair marcelled, straightened, plastered against my skull. One week later, I admitted to myself that the marcel was deceptive, promising more than it delivered. My hair looked soft and waved, yet close up the waves looked phony, manmade-molded as one might form crevasses and creases in clay. My hair wasn't even soft; it was hard, lying motionless against my scalp like a corpse. Most damning of all, I was confronted all week with the most severe disappointment—the status supposedly conferred upon the marcel wearer, was denied me.

To be sure, I fabricated a sense of well-being, convincing myself that I was no longer ugly as I swaggered and threw back my head: did I expect the hair to fall down around my forehead, to waft in the air? People just stared at me in the streets or during work. Still, after the first few days the old feelings of insecurity returned. The marcel had not, contrary to expectations, made me more attractive to women, white or mulatto. In fact, most of those whom I propositioned seemed to be mocking me, first for my being me, now second for my wearing a marcel. My relatives said nothing about my new hair style, though I sensed their displeasure. Their way, however, was to pity me, not to be angry with me, for they were perceptive enough to understand that the search for good hair masked a search for something more tangible. Their perception, as I read it then, caused me to re-examine, in a small way, tangibles which had led me to efface myself in an attempt to buy security, an identity. I did not then arrive at any conclusions regarding the whys and wherefores, would not allow myself to recognize the tangibles, but I concluded that I would no longer rely upon gimmickry, that I would equal the mulattoes, force them to accept me, to recognize me, by the strength of my own accomplishments. For an entire week—two weeks after having my hair marcelled—I washed it each night with soap and water. At the end of three weeks, all traces of the marcel gone, I went back to my notebook and typewriter.

There were experiences to come which would bring about greater awareness, one in particular which would push me closer to that barricade across the other side of which, hidden, cringing, lay myself . . .

My encounter with Phoebe, a mulatto barmaid, would not only inadvertently send me scurrying, suitcase in hand, to board yet another Greyhound bus, but more importantly, it would restore a sense of my own self-worth, help me to realize that the myths by which I had lived, now for twenty-three years, were unfounded, that my mulatto-phobia existed almost completely in my own mind. Had I not needed for my own sanity, my own protection, to view women as abstractions, Phoebe might have also helped me to view mulattoes and women realistically, not as phantoms, but as human beings. Even the attempt to dare this, however, lay some years in the future, for now, as when a child, wracked by conflicting feelings about the madonna, I had few options about what perception I could formulate about women. I necessarily dealt with them as non-human, as romantic abstractions, lest I be forced to think of them in derogatory terms, to be ashamed of them even, to hate them, to see them as symbols of past symbols, to be wrenched with pity on the one hand and torn by outrage on the other.

I met Phoebe, whose skin was whiter than white, one night after secluding myself in my room and working on a manuscript. I had temporarily put fiction aside—Newark was the setting I had chosen for the novel. But to think of Newark was to think of Yvonne. This, I dared not do! Thus, I moved on to prose, to essays, intending to return to fiction, once the affair with Yvonne was forgotten. They were innocuous pieces which served mostly to help me rationalize my isolation from my friends and relatives. The themes of each were basically similar, dealing with loneliness, struggle, eventually success in overcoming all obstacles. Bogged down in the middle of one such essay, I had walked over to the bar some five blocks from my rooming house to sit alone as usual, drinking. During the nights I had come to the bar, I had not remained impassive to the shapely barmaid, but had been wary of approaching her. She was, after all, a mulatto, who moved with a sense of assurance. Well-dressed customers, with their Buicks and Cadillacs waiting outside, were forever propositioning her, buying her drinks, fussing over her. She flirted with them, but eluded their advances, seemed unimpressed by their talk of money and women, brought them free drinks only after they had purchased a number at the bar.

On that night, however, I had purchased only one drink, not yet finished, and had no intention of buying another, when she unceremoniously set another drink before me. "I didn't order another drink," I said, ready to pay, nevertheless.

"I know," she said, "this one's on me. Call me when you finish it." She danced toward the other end of the bar, began pouring a refresher for another customer.

I looked after her, finished the first drink, toyed with the second, wondered. She was back fifteen minutes later, filling my glass again. She leaned across the bar: "Why you always coming in here with that hangdog look?"

"What kind of look is that?" I asked, wondering still about the drinks.

"Like one of them with a long face, hanging down all the time; like he gonna cry." A customer entered, signaled her. She waved him to a halt, stood staring at me. I laughed cautiously, turned my eyes to the ceiling, became emboldened, said, "What do they do with hang dogs in your country?"

She stared back through smiling brown eyes. "Either you shoot it or you pat it on the head."

I asked carefully, still uncertain, "Which one are you going to do to me?"

She brushed a strand of hair away from her forehead, placed a white hand on my arm, whispered seductively, "Come back at three o'clock and find out." She moved off down to the other end of the bar. Immediately I began to reflect, to analyze. Three o'clock was closing time and she wanted me to come back to meet her. Why? Did she believe that she could get money from me? Was she mad with her boyfriend? She was a "bar lady." She wore expensive clothes, had a mature look about her face which added years to her age. She walked with assurance and talked with certainty. She was mulatto, more white and more beautiful than any of those in Newport News. And she wanted me to meet her. Why? I finished my drink, reeled slightly toward the door. Above the noise of the jukebox, she called out, "Don't you forget me, now."

I was embarrassed because the other patrons turned to look directly at me; someone laughed. They know, I thought. They are all part of this game, this charade. I should not go back. I should go home to my typewriter, then to bed. But at home, I could neither write nor sleep. The words came, jumbled and unclear. When I gave up out of frustration, and stretched across the bed, I could not sleep. I sat on the side of the bed, smoked a cigarette, moved toward the bathroom down the hall, back again, lit another cigarette. I sat watching the smoke spiraling, blue, black, fading finally into gray misty walls and the smoke and the drinks, the stuffiness, the closeness of my room gave me the courage to think of other times, and the courage also to fantasize. Phoebe was not simply a symbol, she was the authentic article, the dream desired. "Light, bright and not damn near white," but white, she was what men, dark like me, had striven for, had desired, still desired. Phoebe, for a wife, a girl friend, a mistress, conferred instant status; she was more valuable than a white woman, because she was safer and because, in most cases, she was more beautiful. As a young boy, I might dream of Alice and Doretha, but never of a Phoebe, never one so close to white. No, she belonged not to those like me, but to men with patched-sleeve coats, open convertibles, fine homes with gardens out front, white men or light tanned men, men with wavy hair.

And I was afraid of her, as I had been afraid of Doretha and Alice, had not wanted them to mock me because of my ugliness, had believed always that I was not good enough for them. I did not dare dream that they might do anything beyond notice me, was happy if one of them smiled at me, was nice to me. Now, however, I could at least dream, fantasize. Yes, I dreamed the dream of the hopeful wake, we would meet at three o'clock, and she would come back with me to this one room, with the lumpy bed and cardboard closet, the bureau with the cracked mirror. Yes, she would do this because she was one of those mulattoes who had gone mad, who craved sex with dark black men, a veritable whore, waiting to put out for the asking. And she would put out to me, I dreamed.

I would guide her to the bed, offer her a drink; later, I would kiss her, softly first, then bruisingly. I would fondle her large breasts, run my hands across the nipples, move my hands slowly up her legs, brush against the crotch of her panties, linger there, then move on to caress her stomach.

We would have established a rhythm by then, and she would slide out of her clothes as I continued to caress her, slide out of her dress, slip, down to her panties, and I would fix my eyes on her light tan skin, almost white in the semi-darkness, no, white. I would marvel at it, would watch, fascinated still, as she slid out of her panties, becoming all white now, save for the hedgerow of brown between her legs. And I would be inside of all that whiteness, pummeling it, punishing it, hurting it, forcing it to call out, no, to shout out my name!

As usual, my dreams and fantasies were unfilled. Phoebe did not sleep with me the first night, or the second, or the third. The first night we talked of homes away from home—she was from Arkansas. Then we talked about ambitions—she had wanted to be a model—about my writing, about the reading she did—she read Black writers, Richard Wright, Chester Himes, Willard Motley—about her job and the strange people she met. By our third meeting, three weeks later, she talked about herself, about men, her life now.

Being a mulatto in America, I discovered with great surprise, was as difficult as being Black. If you were a mulatto woman, Phoebe had talked honestly, other Blacks did not trust you, assumed that you thought you were better than they were, primarily because *they* thought that you were, and the whites always felt threatened, thought that you wanted something from them, their men, their positions, their racial status. What, she would ask, if you wanted nothing from whites, wanted only to be identified with Blacks, knew that the white people did not differentiate? Other Blacks looked upon you suspiciously as a freak, wanted to use you before you, as they saw it, could use them. Men wanted to use you either to bolster their own status as men, or to make you into a whore, to strike back at whatever, with a white or light skin, had once hurt them.

If you were a mulatto woman, she emphasized, not without causing me a pang of discomfort, everybody regarded you as a whore. "The white men think that you are one, their wives think so; and the Black men, if they don't get to you in time, they think so too. They always think that they have to buy you, or brutalize you, Black men and white men too, and so you try not to be bought, want to make your own way, but if you are weak enough, soon you allow yourself to be bought, to be possessed."

I sat, almost numbed, surely shocked. She had, as she admitted, been bought and paid for—she was the mistress of one of Philadelphia's most notorious Black gangsters, and she was, she admitted freely, a kept woman. She did not try to rationalize her situation, or apologize for it; that, she had related, was the way things were. I thought of Tillie and wondered what had happened to her, to Red Drag, and the others, mused that I was out of touch even with the people I knew. I sat staring at Phoebe as she talked, glad that she spoke, slowly, steadily, so that I did not have to answer, able to move in and out of my own thoughts. I could no longer see her, as I had seen Yvonne, as an abstraction; she was unlike any woman I had known—honest, not condescending, troubled, but not overwhelmed. She did not need or want a savior,

I knew, could have been saved a long time ago, but wanted something very much like peace, a respite, maybe, from chaos. She was as strong as she was beautiful, had looked across the barricade at herself, had not flinched, had looked and decided that she would, at least for now, accept what she was, with no apology, with few regrets.

When that moment arrived, therefore, when we were ready to climax our fondness for one another through the ritual of sex, when we had both become sure of our feelings toward one another, it was not she who faltered but I—I who was haunted by the demons of old, who was warring still with shadows. Twice, softly, she had called my name as I tenderly caressed her legs, kissed her burnished white breasts. She had waited, I knew, for me to move onward, to press my body upon hers, wanting, desiring the commingling of these two branches from the same racial tree, the uniting of Black and yellow/white bodies in defiance of the taboos of both our childhoods. I wanted another drink. I wanted to get up and walk around. There was a fire somewhere in my head, my breast, cold then hot, causing my body to tremble, searing at my insides. "I have never slept with a mulatto before," I thought in panic, trembling, faltering; I went limp, as if somehow my organ had wilted, was no longer there, had folded up somewhere inside of me.

The thought would not go away. "I have never made love to a mulatto before!" Desperately, I kissed her breasts again, fondled her legs, touched the space between them. No use. The light streaming in from the street outside continued to illuminate her body, so that even as she lay expectantly beneath me, even as the dream bordered upon reality, I was frightened, confused.

I do not know how much of all of this she understood, whether she divined the real source of my pain. But she called out softly, "Wait," and bringing her hands under my buttocks, easing me off her, she slid me onto my back. "Be still." She lay beside me, on her stomach, stroked my legs, my buttocks, kissed my lips. "Wait." Her hands exploded over my body, and she moved her body closer to mine, even closer, and her fingers kneaded my leg muscles, my arm muscles, folded/unfolded the flesh around my stomach, and the kisses came quickly, wetly, on my eyes, my lips, again, again, and so I knew even then that I could down fear, that I could confront the past, stare it away, drown out the voices of

old, for on the seventh day I arose from the dead, threw myself
from the moldy coffin, stepped out into the bright warmth of
light and air, a brave new man in a brave new world, and the
drums of ages past sounded their chant to the living, as two bodies, race of the same race, cleaved apart by the diaspora, were com-
mingled in a cacophony of sound, of laughter, of pleasure, of
beauty, of life.

"You look so peaceful," she said much later, laying on her
stomach, her right hand tracing the veins on my arm.

"I feel so peaceful," I replied, hoping that this short statement
might substitute for what I could not bring myself to tell her. For
the first time in my life, I had made love without guilt or shame or
anger, for the first time had not seen the face of the madonna
before me or beneath me, had not been the many men, not
wanted to be them. I had been free to give, to feel, to love with
tenderness, not pain, with compassion, not hurt. And for the first
time since Tillie, I had made love not with an idea, but with a
woman, had thought of her as such, had felt the womanness of
her, smelled it, tasted it. Peaceful? Yes, mine was the tranquillity
of the lost cub, secure once again in his natural habitat, the
peacefulness which comes with understanding and contentment
and, though I did not know it then—neither of us did—I was not
to find such contentment again for a very long time.

There was so much that we did not know then: we did not
know, especially, that ours was to be only a winter's love, though
perhaps we suspected it, for we lived that winter as if it would, indeed, be our last. Years later, while reviewing a book by my contemporary Askia Toure, a poet with a poet's romantic vision of
the world, I was to recall my winter with Phoebe, become nostal-
gic. "Let it be summer," Askia had written, but smilingly I had
mumbled under my breath, "No, let it be winter. Let it be winter
in Philadelphia. Let there be snow covering the dingy shanty-like
houses along the South Side, painting the neat brownstones,
packed together like hungry lovers, a gleaming white. Let there be
the snow of winter, covering our footsteps as we walked downtown streets together, and let this winter's snow shower upon us
from the elevated train, fall into our eyes, as Phoebe, following my
cue, gazes also at some tall building, jostling with the sky. Yes, let
it be the winter of brown eyes staring out at me, sad sometimes,
alive most of the time, staring out at me with love, with ten-

derness, as I read from pieces of my novel, from an essay, from a poem; and let it be the winter when the boy finally almost achieved manhood, almost found a reason, a meaning, for being; yes, let it be winter."

We discovered soon enough, that the seasons, too, were deceptive. They ended.

The winter season was almost over, the snow having long since disappeared from the streets, the rawness from the air. She had sat on the side of the bed, staring at me, doing what she had to do, donning the guise of the dreaded messenger. What else was there to say? The winter was for children. We were adults. As always with adults, the inevitable had occurred. Frank Reynolds had moved to reclaim his property. He was a big man in Philadelphia, a man of much property. He owned the biggest Black numbers bank, bars, houses of prostitution, two homes, three cars, policemen, a wife, and Phoebe. A giant of a Black man, his very presence intimidated. He owned all of these things. Exclusively. He wanted Phoebe back. He had everything and I had nothing; still, he wanted Phoebe back!

"As long as it was like I didn't care too much," she said, "he was all right. But he knows how much I like you. He was making love to me the other night and I was thinking about you. I called your name. He got mad. He slapped me, said he would kill me. Then he said he would kill you, instead." Her hands moved caressingly atop mine. "He would too."

I halted my cigarette in midair, gestured toward the bed, shouted, almost hysterically, "Fuck Reynolds." I moved my hand from hers, folded my fingers into a tight ball, flailed the air. "You hear me, fuck Reynolds."

She reached for my hand again, caressed it: "I don't want to see you hurt. Oh, lord, I don't want to see you hurt. You don't know that man. He won't do nothing to you himself. But there are three hundred bums out there would kill you even if they thought he wanted you dead."

Even the rage did not cloud my comprehension. I knew enough about Frank Reynolds to know that all she said was true. He could have me killed with no trouble, in such a way that no one would know that I was dead. He was not only respected in the Black community, he was feared as well. I moved closer to her on the bed, placed my hand on her cheek: "We could go to New York—together."

She kissed my hand, softly. "No, I can't. You have too."

Realization took the place of rage. Of course she couldn't go. What kind of choice would that be? Me for Frank Reynolds? How absurd. I was sorry that I had even asked her, sorry, too, that I had brought such misery into her life. Had I been a famous writer, I could have offered a choice worthy of her, could have taken her from this egomaniacal old man. I placed my arms around her and began to cry. Soon we were both crying, together. "There were," I was to write in my journal, many years later, "for us, no more winters. Seasons were for the very young. They came and went and one had to catch them, hold them, only for the moment. Summer? No, Askia, my friend, not summer, but winter. Let it be winter in Philadelphia. Let it be winter wherever Phoebe might be; yes, let it be winter; if not always, then sometimes."

CHAPTER 5

I arrived in New York in 1955, five days before my twenty-third birthday, despondent, but not overly depressed. The sadness that accompanied my leaving Yvonne had not afflicted me when I left Phoebe. I was hurt, disappointed, but I was not immobilized. Able to look upon our condition, I saw our experiences as part of a natural order of things. She had, I suppose, imbued me with something of her pragmatism, helped me to understand that all things, particularly the private and the very personal, were tenuous, could not last, but that in the very tenuousness of things lay their value, their worth. I could not, then, completely understand the meaning of our experience, was to learn only later what I suppose she knew already with that Goethe whom I had yet to read, that the important aspect of the human condition is that one capture the moment, the hour, treat it as if it were eternity itself.

I was able, somewhat now, to deal with the private and the personal, but in New York, I would be confronted with the world outside, in ways that I had never been before. I would be forced for the first time to understand complex human relationships, those between Blacks and whites, which, heretofore, had been overly simplified for almost everyone I had known, except my father. For New York, the city of mythology, which, even as a boy, listening to the tales of soldiers, hustlers, summer visitors, I and others thought of as the epitome of the melting pot, the proof of the thesis of the multiracial city in operation, proved to be little more than delusive.

Living in Harlem for the first four months after my arrival on 135th Street and Eighth Avenue, down the hill from the City College of New York, I discovered the metaphor for the myth, the prime example of the delusion under which New Yorkers lived. My first job was as an orderly at Long Island College Hospital, in downtown Manhattan. The bus which transported me there ran through Harlem, down on the East Side, past Ninety-sixth Street, into City Hall. Both whites and Blacks were on the bus coming from downtown, from City Hall, but as the bus passed beyond Ninety-sixth Street, the riders became either Black or Puerto Rican. There were, I discovered, no laws or rules such as had existed in Virginia indicating separation of the races. Indeed, every law, every phrase of rhetoric from New York politicians and writers, conveyed exactly the opposite. Yet here was the solid, visible evidence that separation was maintained, however enforced I did not then know.

But the discrimination was secondary to the hostility. Once outside of Harlem, away from other Blacks, I was to discover that the hostility of whites was undisguised, open. Clerks in downtown stores eyed me suspiciously whenever I walked in, panic visible in their faces, their eyes following me about the store. White men with their women, when confronting me on the street, pulled them close protectively. Even in Harlem, the hostility toward Blacks was not abated. Walking into the corner drugstore one midday, looking for hand lotion, finding none, and about to walk out, I was accosted by the owner: "You gon pay for that bottle you got in your pocket?" he asked. He was a short, arrogant, white man, big nose, red bloodstained eyes behind silver rimmed glasses.

"What damn bottle?" I asked angrily.

"The one you took off the counter."

I walked over, emptied my pockets, looked into the bloodstained eyes. "You see any damn bottle?"

Nervously, he backed away behind the counter. He was not about to admit to me, Black, that he had made a mistake. "Well," he whispered, "that's all right, but I saw you take it."

I threw up my hands in disgust and walked out of the store.

The hostility was visible also on the jobs in which I worked, three different orderly jobs in three years, among the workers and the patients alike. There was no such outward hostility as that of

Mrs. Martin in Philadelphia; for New Yorkers to utter the word "nigger" in my presence would have been unthinkable. Their vocabulary consisted of "them" and "they," "those people." Doctors, patients, interns, white maids and orderlies issued their euphemisms, talking of "those people on welfare," or "those people who commit all the crimes," those people who made New York unlivable.

I listened to them then, something in later years I would not bother doing, and felt a sense of elation, momentarily, that I was being distinguished from the others, singled out. Soon, however, I began to withdraw from them, to hate whites for their hypocrisy; and I began also to hate other Blacks who condescended to them as I had done in years past, who obsequiously sought their friendship. White people were now beginning to invade my consciousness as never before. They replaced the mulattoes as arch villains in all of my writings. I shifted the theme and focus of my novel primarily, I suppose, because of Phoebe, and made my hero a warrior not so much against mulattoes, but against whites. I saw them now, as the main obstacle to overcome, the Waterloo, which I had to confront. Subsequent experiences, three years after my arriving in New York City, would establish them as major, eternal antagonists.

In the spring of 1958, I changed my occupation from orderly to porter, secured a job at the Brooklyn Army Base, and moved to another Brooklyn neighborhood—my third since moving to Brooklyn from Harlem some two years before. Six months later, I met Elizabeth, shopping in the stores along Myrtle Avenue, close to my apartment. She had been one of the most sought after mulattoes in Virginia. The offspring of a white father and a Black mother, she was almost as white as Phoebe, and she possessed still the body which as a teen-ager had caused old men and young alike to drool, to hunger. She had graduated from Huntington the year I entered and though I often spoke to her while passing in the street, she was so far beyond those like me, because of her complexion, that I worshiped her only from afar.

She had blossomed into complete womanhood during the intervening years, and when I met her in New York, she was beautiful, imposing. The first time I sighted her, I went over and introduced myself. She had frowned, a cold, distant look coming to her face; she shook me off, said she did not know me. I met her three times after that, tried to jolt her memory. Each time she stared at me with contempt, feigned ignorance, became annoyed. On the last occasion, anxious to prove that I was not a molester—and she had made me feel as if I were one—I had walked to keep up with her as she moved rapidly down the street, calling out names of mutual friends, Alice, Lloyd, William, the names of streets on which we had passed each other, Marshall, Jefferson, Roanoke. Suddenly she stopped, turned, glowered at me, shouted: "Look, I don't know you and you better leave me alone, hear?" My arms were outspread in supplication, my lips moved but no words came, I looked ashamedly from the face of one spectator to another. Elizabeth continued walking, turned the corner, and rushed downstairs to the basement of her apartment house.

Two nights later, as I walked down the street on which she lived, two men emerged from the building, rushed past me, their footsteps making staccato-like sounds upon the concrete. "The sonofabitch got a gun," one had said to the other in passing. Frightened by the idea of being caught in a cross fire, not sure of what the situation was, instinctively I began to run in the opposite direction from the others, down to the Brooklyn Hospital, my initial destination. Three cops took me bodily, roughly from the emergency ward.

I was ushered into a precinct station in Brooklyn and made to sit, still handcuffed, in a chair at a desk. The man on the other side of the desk did not look like a policeman. He wore a rumpled pinstriped suit, a grayish white shirt with a red and blue checkered tie. He was not as tall or as heavy as the man who stood next to me on my right. This man had soft, warm eyes; with a tinge of sadness in his voice he said, "C'mon now, the lady and her husband are coming down here, they gonna tell us you tried to break into their house. Admit it, be a man."

Frightened, I blurted out the story of the two men, looked at the cop to my right, said, "I didn't try to break into that house."

I did not see the blow coming. Even after the open palm smashed into the side of my face, forcing me to reel in the chair, throwing me into numbed dizziness, even when, handcuffed, I groped toward the desk, strained to hit back at the white man behind the desk, even after the man on my right pushed me ruthlessly back into my chair, I was not certain from which one the blow had come. The hostile tones of the cop behind the desk revealed him as the assailant: "Goddammit, nigger. You and your goddamn friends tried to break into that house. Didn't ya?" The other cop pinned my manacled arms behind my back, paining me. I shook with anger, fright, rage. The cop moved from behind the desk, to a position in front of me, brought his face close to mine, "All right, let's have it, the truth."

I shook my head no. This time I did not have to speculate about where the blow had come from. I watched him arch his body, lean over precipitously, deliberately, take aim. I saw the wispy brown hairs on his white fingers just seconds before the open palm crashed once again against the side of my face.

Elizabeth and her husband were brought into the room, and through dazed, tear-filled eyes, I looked at her, my apprehension and fear beginning to grow. The two cops ignored me, began talking to Elizabeth's husband, a dirty-colored mulatto. "You got a gun?"

Answer: "Yeah, a shotgun."

"You should've shot the bastard."

Answer: "I would have. But by the time I got it, the sonofabitch musta seen my shadow, took off. Otherwise, he wouldn't be sitting here now."

"Too bad," the cop who had been sitting at the desk, now standing to my right, said as he kicked me against the leg.

Elizabeth had looked on in outraged loveliness, waiting for the others to finish their conversation, her blue eyes aglow with excitement and anticipation. "He's been molesting me, almost every day, on the damn street," she said sadly, with consternation. "Almost every day. I can't walk the damn street."

This piteous recitation brought all eyes, enraged, to focus on me, murderous eyes. I stared up at the ceiling, anxious to avoid the eyes of these three angry white men. I was, I knew, the only Black person in that room. The others had far more in common with each other than with me. The detectives were unable to keep their eyes off Elizabeth; since she had entered the room, their eyes had shown me no mercy. It was as though I had been charged with molesting one of their own—she must have been far more beautiful than their wives or mistresses—and the murder which spoke from their eyes was the murder of the lynch mob, the demand for two eyes and more from the dirty Black brute who dared to molest the white chrysanthemum. I startled them by speaking out. "That's not true, Elizabeth. I never molested you. I wanted you to remember."

I received another blow. Partly, I suppose, because of my insolence. More, however, because of my disrespect toward Elizabeth. To attempt to break into her house was one thing; to try to molest her was another; but to sit here, look her in the eyes, and call her name, familiarly, in the presence of white men, was the supreme crime. I knew, when I had spoken out, that it was not a question of whether I would be hit again or not, but a question of who would get to me first, who would try to ram the words of protestation down my throat, who would be the first to demonstrate to this woman of mixed blood the extent to which white men were willing to go to protect her honor.

When they finally released me, I was remanded to a cell for the remainder of the morning, and the next day brought into court. The judge, a tired-looking man in black glasses, seemed uninterested in either me or the court. He listened nonchalantly as the detective read off the charges against me, listened with equal disdain as Elizabeth's husband described the events of the night, concluding with, "I chased the suspect down to Brooklyn Hospital. When I saw him go into the hospital, I flagged down a squad car."

They were determined to nail down the case against me, had brought their own lawyer. He was a pompous-looking brown-skinned man in a tweed suit who, when glancing in my direction, appeared to sense something dirty, repulsive. "Your honor," he said, "we want this man put away. He's been hounding this woman for the last year. [I had only become conscious that Elizabeth lived in the neighborhood three months ago.] He has assaulted her with abusive language, followed her up and down the street, made threats. And now this—trying to break into her house, to rob her—or—something else . . ."

The "something else" was more a statement than a question. I tried to interrupt, said "I didn't . . ."

The judge cut me off. "Wait a minute, young man," he said, kindly, "you'll have your chance."

The tone of his voice inspired hope. Of all the people gathered about the stand, he regarded me, it seemed, with the least hostility. He seemed unimpressed by Elizabeth's beauty. He turned from me and called upon the assistant district attorney, a tall mulatto with a pencil mustache beneath his upturned nose. He appeared at Elizabeth's side, glowered over at me: "The charges are serious, your honor. Attempted breaking and entering, plus molesting. There've been several crimes of this sort in that area. He was caught and identified by these people."

Seemingly unimpressed, the judge turned to me. "How do you plead, young man?"

I astounded everybody. "I'm not guilty!" I said.

I was to learn later that I was expected to enter a guilty plea. They believed that I was a criminal and they expected me to act like one. They thought that I was sophisticated enough to know that if you are a first offender, there is no sentence except for a serious crime. Had I been knowledgeable of white justice, therefore, as everyone assumed that I was, I would have pleaded guilty, copped a plea, thrown myself on the mercy of the court. Out of sheer ignorance of the fine points of the law, I pleaded not guilty.

Bail was set for me at five hundred dollars, and I was taken back to the house of detention, where I remained until a friend managed to post bail. During the time between then and my next scheduled court appearance, I hired a lawyer. On the first date set for trial, the complainants did not appear. On the next date, Elizabeth appeared with her lawyer, and they held conversations with mine. I never knew what they talked about, but the case was dropped. Once in conversation with my white lawyer, I had told him how the police had beaten me. He had sighed, shaken his head: "I know. They always beat colored boys. And there's not a damn thing anybody can do about it."

Three weeks later, when I was able to look back upon the events of that time with a perception unclouded by rage and anger, I was confronted with what remained throughout my life, a serious contradiction. I had been brutalized by white men, to be sure, but other white men had treated me kindly, the judge, my lawyer. It had happened, before—I recalled Donald—and it would happen again, and I did not know then how I would deal with it. All were defined by the same common denominator, all were white, but their actions seemed to differentiate them from one another. How then to tell the villain from the good guy, the white madman from the conscientious white? I tried working out the conundrum in essay after essay, tearing up one piece after another. One year after the incident with Elizabeth, another, less dramatic but equally cathartic incident supplied me with a partial answer.

Years after, in my first book, *The Black Situation,* I was to write about this incident in some detail, in essay form. Two days after it happened, however, I jotted it down, briefly, in the form of a drama. Characters: me and a white employer. Setting: a restaurant in lower Manhattan.

> Me, handing white employer a card, saying: "I was sent by the Gold employment agency about the job you listed."
> White employer, ignores the card, scowls, blurts out: "Why did they send you? We don't hire Negroes."
> Me, consternation on my face, surprise; not hurt yet, not angry. I look at the card in my hand, read the message: "Job Description: Porter. Three years experience at the Brooklyn Army Base. Good references. Excellent at the job of sweeping floors."
> White employer, moving a few feet away from me, concern now spreading across his face: "I'm sorry. They shouldn't have sent you. There's a mistake. Let me give you your carfare."
> Me, balling up my fists, snarling at him: Curse, turn, walk away from his outstretched hand.
> Curtain.

The incident helped to resolve my confusion concerning whites, made me realize that despite the fact that there were such people as Donald, the judge, the lawyer, others with whom I had come in contact, I could not afford to look at them as individuals. If only for my own protection, I had to see them en masse. It was, I wrote in an essay, as if a group of hired assassins were after me, and they all wore dark clothes with black masks, and were in a crowd of other people, also clothed in dark clothes and black masks. I could not then afford to speculate upon which was the real and genuine, which was the fake. I needed to protect myself as best I could from them all, adopting a defensive stance toward all. After all, I concluded the essay, the genuine assassins outnumbered the counterfeit by about fifty to one.

Taken together, however, the two incidents convinced me of

how vulnerable I was, not only to whites, but to Blacks like Elizabeth and her husband, their lawyer, and the district attorney. This had nothing to do with the fact that they were mulatto; since Phoebe, I had almost overcome my mulatto-phobia. But, as middle-class people, they had regarded me with the same derision as the whites, had perhaps not beaten me only because they were in no position to do so. I thought of my father and his often repeated declaration of the connivance between Blacks and whites, and I understood something of the symbiotic relationship existing between Black middle class and whites. For the most part, they were distinguishable only by the difference in skin color. They shared the same values, the same wants, needs, and much the same opinion of Blacks like myself.

It was as though I had been transported again to Newport News, lined up against Blacks who often looked at me, as Elizabeth's lawyer had looked at me, with repulsion, denying by their very glances my right to exist. But I was no longer a child, and the anger and rage of the past, exemplified in the courage I had displayed by standing up for myself in the courtroom, prevented me any longer from accepting the role of villain. I knew I would continue to write, continue to send out poems, essays, shorts stories, receive rejection slips; but I would also, until I published something, work at such orderly and porter jobs, leaving myself vulnerable to Blacks and whites alike. Most of all, I knew I would not achieve that victory over that growing list of my enemies which I hungered for unless I set higher immediate goals for myself. This realization drove me in 1960, at the age of twenty-eight, to enroll in college, in the City College of New York.

My five years at the college—two as a part-time student at night, three as a full-time day student—are chronicled in the diary I kept for the full period. The diary constituted an inconclusive record; there was little of life itself; recorded were only the bare statistics of struggle. Notations about the process of overcoming ten years' absence from school predominated:

June 15, 1962
Dear Diary:
Have finished *War and Peace*. Tolstoi is lively, informative, argumentative. Began reading *Reprieve*, by Sartre.

June 18, 1962
Dear Diary:
Summer school has begun. Homework for economics.
Exam Scheduled. I may as well be taking German as
Chaucer's Old English. Finished *Reprieve*. Did not like
Sartre.

June 21, 1962
Dear Diary:
Am behind in economics, may not come out too well.
Will probably do fine in English.

August 16, 1963
Dear Diary:
Seven exams to go. Had Bio exam tonight—don't think
I did too well.

August 15, 1963
Dear Diary:
The semester is almost over. Four weeks remaining.
Sevens exams, B on my English paper. Working doubly
hard, worried about biology, rereading Kafka, feel that
I'm way behind . . . mentally exhausted.

August 22, 1963
Dear Diary:
It looks hopeless. Think I failed another exam tonight.
Did not even do well on my speech. Another Bio exam
tomorrow.

August 23, 1963
Dear Diary:
Disaster. Think I did bad on another Bio exam. Can
count only sixteen right answers out of forty. Everything
is going wrong. Heading for my worst semester.

August 24, 1963
Dear Diary:
Second 80 of the semester—82—on an art exam. First A
of the semester—on my English paper. Only Biology
stands between me and a miracle.

August 30, 1963
Dear Diary:
Bio exam results. Not completely disastrous. 67 on the practicum—not bad, not good, still stand a chance for a C.

June 4, 1963
Dear Diary:
Long semester is over. Not too bad. B in English, B in Health, A in Speech, C in Art, C in Biology.

There were the despondent times, the despairing times, all recorded economically, devoid of real feeling or emotion:

June 29, 1962
Dear Diary:
Terribly depressed today. Angry, fighting with everyone. Terribly agitated, I don't know why.

July 3, 1962
Dear Diary:
Confusion! Where am I going? What do I want? Why do things bother me so much? Why am I so unhappy?

November 29, 1962
Dear Diary:
Still depressed for most of the day. Wrote one of my most beautiful poems. About death. Feel much better, now.

January 1, 1963
Dear Diary:
New Year's day. Confusion raging inside of me. Seem to be living in tension day by day. Am beginning to feel very lonely.

July 2, 1963
Dear Diary:
Can't sleep. Awake all night. Depressed. Not studying very well. Think I want to cry.

People move in and out of the pages, names, bringing with them, sometimes, faces, shapes: Mr. Gershenson, my supervisor in the pharmacy at Sydenham Hospital, where I worked part time, a kindly man, intellectual, joining with Mr. Legande and Mr. Branch, to buy me books each semester, encouraging me, inspiring me. Mel, destined to commit suicide, helping me over the few rough years, helping me to understand my own talents, my own gifts. Dr. Rosenthal, teacher, young, bright, impressed by my writing and reading, convincing me to change my major to literature. Professor Manson, teacher of the Victorian period, old, wise, giving me a copy of Browning, inscribing it. Dr. Berger, dean, counselor, becoming a lifetime friend, lauding my accomplishment in those last years, reminding me of how far I had come. Dr. Karl, professor, encouraging me to study English, reading my novel, pushing me to apply for a scholarship to graduate school. James Emmanuel, poet, my only Black professor, later, colleague, confidant, friend.

There were the names of women, also, students and nonstudents, people who drifted in and out of my life, some making indelible impressions, recurring again and again in the diary, some appearing only once. Incidents of the sixties, the Meredith experience, the Cuban Missile Crisis, the bombing and killing of four children in Birmingham, the assassinations of Kennedy and Malcolm X are noted, recorded, registered without seeming emotion. This was not because the incidents, each of them, did not lead me to anger, tears, or rage, but only because I could not allow myself to be distracted by them, could not become so obsessed with the drama of the sixties that I would forsake what, for me, was my life-saving preoccupation.

I would never live down my sense of guilt concerning my nonparticipation, besides attending a few rallies, a few lectures, in the struggle of the sixties. I was keenly aware that decisive events were being made, that the sit-inners and freedom riders, courageous young people and adults, were stepping outside of history and confronting American society as never before. I praised their actions, worried about their deaths, wrote poems and essays about their gallant struggles; beyond this, I could not, would not go. Being so engaged, so preoccupied with my private war, I could not wholeheartedly join the other, though I was well aware that that, too, was my war.

Moreover, I steadily gained the confidence in myself to believe that I could win my own war, emerge victorious over my enemies.

Each term paper praised, each examination passed, each course successfully completed, produced a belief in the possibility of greater success. The attention of teachers and students, the recognition, at last, that I was a bright young man, spurred me to greater belief in myself, in my own potential. Jackie Robinson's kind words concerning my second novel, which I finally completed, enhanced my self-esteem, and a visit home, during my last year in college, helped even more.

One day after finishing my novel, during the summer of 1961, I had impulsively called Jackie Robinson's office. I did not know him, but I knew he had a reputation for helping other Blacks, and that he had published a book of his own. I called his Chock Full O'Nuts office, surprised when he answered his own telephone. Nervously, I asked if he could, perhaps, read my novel, comment upon it. He had urged me to mail it to him, and three weeks later, I received his encouraging reply: "I think this is good and should be published. I will send it to some people I know. One thing, though; I think you should change the ending. We don't want people to think that we are seeking revenge."

I was not very hopeful, not very expectant, kept my fantasies to a minimum, convinced myself that the manuscript would not be accepted so that the disappointment would not be so overwhelming. I was prepared, therefore, when, some two months later, after he had sent the book to several publishers, he returned it to me with a letter in which he wrote, "I hope to read one day that you have published it."

From time to time now, I take the novel from among stacks of old manuscripts, discarded, but not to be thrown away. Rereading portions of it, I understand why it was rejected. It was an improvement over the first novel, but, despite this, very bad. The characters were wooden, had no life. Whatever action there was, took place in long-drawn-out soliloquies. The organization was chaotic and confusing. A great deal of reading had gone into the book. Richard Wright was there; so, too, was Dostoevski; there was the imprint of the Frederick Douglass of the autobiography in the Victorian-like language, and the influence, style, and language of a new Black writer, James Baldwin. In addition, I had somewhat changed the plot sequence, eliminated the mulattoes as primary antagonists, substituting whites. I had also changed the major female character from light skin, to Black.

The story line of the *Black Messiah* involved Charles Brown and his girl friend, Berniece. Brown, a tall, Black man with kinky hair and thick lips, is born in a small southern town. From the days of his youth he is abhorred by the Black middle class, who control the institutions in the town with the assent of the whites. Because of his intelligence, his rebelliousness, at the age of sixteen he is arrested on a false charge of rape, beaten, and thrown into jail. The Black middle class, made up of both Blacks and mulattoes, assist the white police in convicting him. Through a contrived sequence, however, someone else confesses to the crime, and Brown, exonerated, is forced to leave town.

Part two of the three-part novel deals with Brown in the North. He becomes involved in a serious love affair, begins to write a novel, and when his girlfriend dies of leukemia, he journeys West in despair. After failing in several attempts to take his own life, he overcomes despondency, completes a novel, which is accepted for publication, and comes back to New York to be hailed as the greatest Black novelist since Richard Wright. Wealth and attention are showered upon him. He makes TV appearances, is sought out for his opinions on the race problem. During one such appearance, he meets Berniece, coal dark in complexion, dark eyes, short hair, pretty, sensitive face. Her love and devotion push him to greater heights. He becomes a major spokesmen for Black people, is lauded as a Negro leader who refuses to make deals with the white enemy. Part two ends with Brown accepted by the masses of Blacks as their leader.

Part three centers around the murder of Emmett Till. When the child is murdered by a white Southerner, Brown, along with establishment Negro leaders, is asked to address an assemblage of Blacks numbering in the thousands. After the establishment leaders have called for patience and restraint, Brown, with Berniece at his side, mounts the speaker's rostrum. Instead of patience and restraint, he advocates revenge, relates to his audience the past of Frederick Douglass and Henry Highland Garnet, urges them to militancy, pushes them to the threshold of violent retribution. The novel ends as Brown and Berniece lead an army of Blacks from New York to Mississippi—their ranks swelling along the way—in a rebellion, uprising against white America.

The book was part autobiographical and part fantasy, and though it was badly written, I was proud of the accomplishment.

I had managed to write three hundred pages, had even dared to analyze aspects of my personal life which years before I would not have dared to think about. Moreover, I had written something that someone else, Jackie Robinson, had read and liked and—despite the fact that the novel itself constituted one more rejection slip from publishers—this alone was enough to inspire me to continue. I had also learned things about myself, not only through the characters and the content of the book, but through the very process of writing itself. I had learned that the isolation, the alienation of my youth, those times when I shut myself away from the world, had given me a pattern which served me well now, and would serve me even better in the coming years. I grew to like solitude, alienation, isolation for its own sake. I had now a rationale for the distance I placed between myself and friends, for the tenuousness, even, of relationships for fear of close, binding contacts. Always in the deep part of my mind was the age-old fear that relationships never lasted, that love was finite, that one would, in the end, be betrayed by those whom he allowed emotionally to move too close. But the discipline required both to write and finish school, pushed such thoughts deeper into my subconscious, and in time I began to see even my manic periods—my highs and lows—as part of the necessary makeup of the writer.

Encouraged by Jackie Robinson's comments on my novel and my success in college—I would finish my undergraduate work in the fall of 1965—I ventured home to Virginia that summer, the first time in thirteen years. I brought with me the marks of my newly acquired status: books already assigned for courses, essays on which I intended to work, a new, portable second-hand typewriter. My mother and the neighbors were outwardly impressed—I was the only one of my family, of the neighborhood, to make it to college, and was petted and fretted over by people who, years ago, had prophesied for me a bad, ignominious end. Some of my old antagonists from Huntington had died or retired, but a few remained, and their carping criticism reached my ears. One such teacher, remembering my earlier days, who had been one of the judges in the oratorical contest, and who had boasted on more than one occasion that she had voted against me, demanded to know from my younger sister, herself then a high school student, how they (my family) ever got money enough to send me to college? Others attributed my being able to remain in college to the fact that the civil rights revolt had pushed whites to accept even Blacks of such caliber as myself, thus attempting to negate my accomplishment. Alice had married and left town, settled somewhere in California, and her father, the wrinkles now showing in his face, treated me politely, yet with the reserve of old. I did not see Alexander or Doretha, but I learned that Alexander had become president of his father's bank and Doretha had been appointed to the faculty of an elementary school. Ollie and Horace had left town, Ollie for Chicago, Horace for Las Vegas, and both were now married and settled.

I visited old, still remembered sights—the garden, which had long since become a housing project. I walked up and down the old neighborhood, from which my mother had moved three years ago. Trailing behind Huntington High School, where the railroad tracks still remained, I wondered what had happened to the children, wondered if they had given the lie to my prophecy. I went alone to Gloucester to visit my father's grave, now covered by weeds, sat as I had sat long ago, thinking not so much about the cars and the noise this time, but about him. I recalled that he had wanted me to be a lawyer, and I wondered what his opinion would be now that I was well on my way to receiving a degree in English literature. He would have been proud, I know, of the storehouse of words I now had at my command, of the thousands of books I had read, but he would have been disappointed that I was not involved in these tumultuous years, that I was not lending my energy or my knowledge to help other Blacks, that the course of study I had chosen did not even point me in that direction.

What, I wondered, would our fights have been about now? Integration, which I had begun to oppose? About the importance of Martin Luther King and Malcolm X? About the changing nature of Newport News itself?

For the city had changed, not so much because of the revolt of the sixties (to this, Newport News had remained almost immune), but in terms of the class and status makeup of the Black population. Mulattoes, like Alexander and Doretha, William and Roger, had moved into professions previously held by their parents; but a majority of the professionals, the schoolteachers, doctors, and lawyers, were Black, not mulatto. The reason was simply that the old mulatto class was dying off and the Korean war had enabled many Blacks, through the GI bill, to attain higher education. Having done so, the civil rights revolt had made them acceptable by whites for jobs previously earmarked for mulattoes.

We would have argued, I knew, about my tendency to isolate myself, my ability to become bored, cold, and distant, never realizing that these had been traits of his, that I had been but a magnificent mimic. But would we have, could we have, any more than before, come to the real issues between us, even recognize them for what they were, come close to understanding them? I thought that we could not. The years had taught me that things were much more complex than I had ever assumed and though I did not know all the complexities, I knew enough to know that at the center of my dispute with him was the madonna. Somehow, this dispute had been at the forefront of much of my rage and anger and had clouded, perhaps forever, my relationship with other women.

Once again, as before, I remained at his graveside until dark, recalling the past, remembering a word, a gesture, a lesson given, a scolding received. When I left the graveside that night, I knew then that I would never return, but I knew also that I would build a monument to him, to us. The second book that I ever published, I promised, would be dedicated to him. The first, I knew even then, would be dedicated to the madonna.

The trip home had allowed me to measure my present self against my past self and once back in New York, I concluded that I liked the present Addison Gayle much better. The patterns of behavior, of reaction, set long ago, were with me still, but I felt, perhaps for the first time in my life, that I had control over my emotions, over those patterns. I had become, certainly, sober, rational, thoughtful, capable of downing the tumult within. Over the past years, I had lost control only once, ventured into the kind of hysteria which had caused me to hurl brick after brick at Walter, which had sent me, back in Newark, to my razor on the dresser.

I know, now, that what had precipitated the incident with Pat had little to with her personally, or with the fact that she was white, Anglo-Saxon white, with shoulder-length brown hair and blue eyes. We had, after all, met in the summer of 1963, had developed a tenuous relationship, had gone to free concerts and movies together, had had sex together many times. I know, too, that my outburst had little to do with her favorable comments concerning my looks, my body, my hair. She had made such comments numerous times before and they had caused me to blush. They had caused me also to recall past years when I thought that the mulattoes made unfavorable comments about physical features.

No, our troubles, or rather mine, had nothing to do with her, but, I believe now, with something over which we had no control, with the incidents taking place in the Black communities in the sixties, and particularly with the bombing death of four Black children in Birmingham, Alabama. Our altercation took place the day following the bombing. I did not know then the extent of the guilt I had felt by becoming a recluse, an outsider, at a time in which it seemed all other Blacks were caught up in a struggle for civil rights. Had I been on the firing line, been involved, I might not have reacted so violently to each setback, might not have gone into despair when the picture of yet another act of brutality flashed across the TV screen. But what I could not give in terms of action, I gave doubly in terms of emotion. I became an armchair warrior, throwing out my curses, spewing out my hatred to the white faces mocking me on the television screen. I empathized with my brothers and sisters, wrote poems about them, wept over their misfortunes.

Had I been more active, I would not, perhaps, have come to view my relationship with Pat as an aberration, a betrayal of those Blacks who were fighting and dying, might not have needed to picture her in my mind as one of the enemy. Yet, on those nights when she would remain overnight in my apartment, when, in the morning, I would arise, see her white face, peaceful, reposed, I would often be filled with shame, with guilt, with contradictory emotions of pity and hate. Why should I distinguish her from the enemy? She had the white skin of the enemy, the blond hair of the enemy, the blue eyes of the enemy. Where would she be, on what side, if she were in Alabama instead of New York, if she were married to Bull Connor or Sheriff Clark?

But moreover, what about me? My politics at that time were not clear, but I was politically leaning toward Black Nationalism, toward Malcolm X and the Muslims. I could be thrown into paroxysms of anguish whenever I viewed a Black woman and a white man together. How could I rationalize my own hypocrisy, explain it to myself? For me, the time-honored rationale that I was "getting back at whitey through fucking his woman" did not work, because while with Pat I did not think of whitey, or of her as whitey's woman. Moreover, I was determined to get back at whitey not through surrogates, but by confronting him, besting him, actually, not symbolically. No, I could never believe that making love to white women compensated for my not taking part in the struggle.

The truth was, however, that I had begun to like her, and as with similar situations to come, I would have to break the relationship, to prevent myself from being closed in, stifled, always to preserve my isolation, my outsidedness. All of this contributed to my emotional harangue that September afternoon of 1963, when we lay, after making love, on our backs. The noonday sun had reached fingerlike, it seemed, through the window, touching our still, half-entwined bodies. Her right hand moved from my shoulder blades down to my buttocks, traced some intricate design on my back. "Your skin," she said, "it's so beautiful. So beautiful."

My muscles tightened at words I had heard before. I rolled away from her quickly, turned over on my back. Starting to leave the bed, I hesitated, scowled at her, feeling my body begin to tremble, my fists to tighten, tasting the anger and sarcasm edging around my words: "The most noble of savages," I said, short, curt, "straight from jungle town."

She managed a half smile, but something in my face must have warned her that this was no comic quip, that danger lay ahead. She recoiled, suddenly, as if from a blow, withdrew her hand rapidly from my forehead. "Look . . . what kind of shit is this?"

I felt her tension and my hostility increased. "From the jungle," I said, "the Black, uncivilized jungle." She bounded from the bed, stood just at its edge, her blue eyes alive with fury. "Goddamn you, Addison Gayle," she shouted, sensing the danger now, "you take that shit somewhere else."

There was sadness in her eyes and I wanted to reach out to her, caress her, explain to her that something was happening and that I did not know what it was; but I could see her now only as a white woman, one of the enemy, and so I struck outward again from the depths of stored-up guilt and hostility: "The white nymph and the Black Othello," I shouted derisively, mocking her one-time description of me as a Black Othello. "How about Black savage?"

She picked up a towel, threw it at me. It landed short, on the side of the bed. "Fuck you," she said, beginning hurriedly to slip into her clothes. "You're crazy, you know. You're sick."

I realize now that I was becoming almost delirious, as her fury increased, as I watched her, so agitated that she had difficulty putting on her shoes, bounced around for a second in bare feet, on one leg, hesitant to sit on the side of the bed. The skin around her eyes and cheeks became flaming red, and as I continued to hurl sarcasm after sarcasm, I skirted close to ethnic insult, veering toward that destination time and again, until finally I reached it, drove home: "Go ahead, Miss Ann," I shouted, almost at the top of my voice. "C'mon, call me a Black nigger. C'mon, baby, say it."

The manic elation was short-lived, disintegrated under her totally confused and panicked state. Beyond her color, now, she resembled the madonna, defeated, beaten, and instantly I was once again in the throes of despair, wanted to take her in my arms, comfort her, protect her from me, wanted to bring back the night before, the times before, wanted to see the light aglow again in her blue eyes.

I never did. We saw each other after that only in passing, avoided taking the same classes with each other. Whenever I did see her, briefly, I noted that the old defiance had gone from her eyes; the sense of self-assurance, of determination, with which she had once seemed to function, too, was gone. I thought of writing her during the weeks of recurring depression, much as I had thought once before of writing my father, of trying to explain all, but I never did. Mentally and emotionally I lacerated myself, secluded myself, began to write and study, not so much to overcome the despondency but only to be able to take respite from it. The despondency, I was beginning to understand now, was a way of compensating for my actions, safer and less demanding than trying to explain them.

There would come a time in the future when I would be able to look upon one such as Pat without the old suspicions, the old myths, the old anxieties. That time would come only when I was able to cross the barricade, come close to understanding something of my real feelings, of my necessity for camouflaging them. I knew then that somehow women were dominating, had always dominated my life, that I was in a sense being defined by them, that only they could crack my wall of isolation. I knew, too, that I needed them to fuel my despair, to maintain me in a world surrounded by enemies. Only later was I to discover that they were also a part of that paranoiac world I had created, that, like Benny, though perhaps without his provocation, I feared them, could only deal with them, once again, as ideas. No, the experiences with Phoebe, had not, as I had thought, wrought such great changes. Since Phoebe, I had had no lasting relationship: that with Pat had lasted longer than most—and my contradictory feelings toward women had remained suppressed. Moreover, I had experienced a freedom in those two relationships that I was not to experience for a long time after. The independence of Phoebe and Pat, their strength of character, their self-confidence, the whiteness of their skins had precluded comparisons with the madonna. (Was this the reason that I had been able to end both of these relationships without going off into deep destructive despondency?) I could not discern the madonna's sadness in their eyes, could not look upon them as being one with the damned.

How much pain might have been avoided, both to myself and to others, had I consciously understood much of this before, had I allowed myself, after Pat, to examine my feelings honestly. Instead, I wallowed in despair for weeks, lacerating myself for my behavior toward her. Although I worked feverishly on school assignments and writing poems and essays, I also looked around, I know now, for another woman, one who could help me expiate my guilt, suffer in atonement.

I though I had discovered her in Ruth. She was black as the berry is black, with long shapely legs, ample bosom, pageboy haircut which enhanced her facial features, Bantu, Negroid. She had the sad, piteous eyes of the madonna, which suggested in their depths, longing and pining. Perhaps she, too, belonged to the legion of the damned, had been beaten, defeated, was unable to wage the intellectual struggle which alone might have saved her. Like Yvonne, like the madonna, Ruth had been victimized by men. She had married at an early age because of an unwanted pregnancy. Later, deserted by her husband and left to care for a child, while still a child herself, Ruth was forced to work long, arduous hours for little pay, forced to protect herself and her child by any means possible. At the age of twenty-six she was a defeated, broken woman.

I attempted to atone for my actions toward Pat—brutal, destructive, I constantly told myself—by pouring out to Ruth all the tenderness I could muster. Night after night I would hold her close, soothe her, comfort her as she cried over misfortune. I came out of my shell of isolation to spend time with her. Together, we went to concerts, to plays in the park, to classes. I advised her on ways of spending her money for the greater benefit of her and her child, lectured her on contraceptives and birth control, read to her from the works of Baldwin, Wright, Proust, and Pasternak, sought her opinions concerning my own writings, and at night, held her tenderly in my arms, cuddling her, cradling her. *Still, I could not save her.*

I remember what was to be our last night together, though I did not know it then. (Did she herself know?) She sat on my windowsill, where Pat had so often sat, looking at the houses silhouetted against the Brooklyn skyline. "Read it again," she said, referring to a passage from Boris Pasternak's *Dr. Zhivago*. I bent my eyes again to the selected passage, read slowly: "Every mother gives birth to a genius. It is not her fault that somewhere along the way, something goes wrong."

She leaned back against the sliver of wall near the window, closed her eyes. "That's nice," she said. Then, "Do you believe it?"

"Yes," I answered, "I do."

She was silent for a moment; then, "You're nice . . . Why are you so nice to me?"

"Because I like you a lot."

"Why should you like somebody like me? You don't want to like nobody like me. I'm no good, I'm subject to have an affair on you anytime. I'm here today, gone tomorrow. I'm twenty-six with a baby and no husband, you ought not to like somebody like me." She had begun to cry again; as always after such an outburst, I rushed to comfort her, repeated: "You're a beautiful person; I love you . . ." The tears had come to my eyes also, the prelude, I knew, to the sweet delirium of despair. I walked to the window, held her in my arms, brought her face down to my shoulder, wiped the tears from the side of her face, listened to her heavy breathing, felt the convulsions of her body, and suddenly *it was as though I were in another time and place and the weeping of the madonna was assaulting my ears, attacking my mind, and I was being driven to hysteria, forced to jam my fingers ruthlessly into my ears, twisting, turning, wanting to stand up, to run away, recalling the lines from my favorite poem, "Thanatopsis," "Yet a few days, and thee the all-beholding sun shall see no more," and suddenly becoming stone deaf to the noises made by the madonna, hearing only the silent sounds of my own crying and screaming, silent echoes of my boyish thought, I love you, I love you.*

After that night, I never saw Ruth again. She vanished, almost spiritlike out of my world. All entreaties of mine, questioning of her relatives, a trip to her home in Camden, New Jersey, availed nothing. She had left the city, suddenly, no one knew where. I began, after a while, to muse over our relationship, trying to discover whatever culpability I had shared for her abrupt departure. I could not believe that she had left without some provocation from me, no matter how slight, could not believe that she would act, as Yvonne had acted before, out of a sense of independence. It didn't seem possible that the reason for her leaving, for not contacting me, had nothing to do with me, but with her. I only knew that in another attempt to "save" another human being, I had failed, and that I had failed to atone for my past transgressions, whatever they might have been. Once again, I sought the relief of despondency.

CHAPTER 6

My experiences with Pat and Ruth remained unanalyzed, primarily, I suppose, because they occurred before I had completely developed what I thought at the time to be a newfound sense of my own worth. The meaning of Jackie Robinson's commentary upon my novel hadn't set in yet, nor had the visit to Virginia and my father's grave. After all this, I became even more self-assured, more aware that I possessed certain strengths and talents. I was, after all, about to graduate from college, and more determined than ever to forbid myself to wander so close to self-pity. I now realized that despair would be a destructive agent. The essays that I wrote after my return home, after Pat and Ruth, dealt with themes of courage, strength, determination. The one short story, written during this period depicted a young man of unbending commitment to his obsession—waging warfare against a hostile society—a commitment which allowed no room for emotion, irrationality. Never before or since was I to write of such a character, of one who purposely conditioned himself to view the world as a rational construction, who had only contempt for the weak and the pitiable. Never again would I equate strength of intellect with strength of character in my writings.

Knowing very little about men—I had not really known my father, would not then truly examine myself—I had patterned this character on what I imagined that I was becoming, on what, out of my fear and anxiety, I wanted to become. Having, I believe, conquered isolation and seclusion, having learned to manipulate despair, I needed now not only to camouflage my feelings, but to replace them with manufactured ones. I needed to protect myself from frequent voyages into the past, from dredging up, out of the labyrinthine corridors of my own mind, all the evidence of past failures. So close now to achieving an important triumph over the past, I needed to exorcise from my mind all past history of weakness. I needed to recapture, with more tenacity than ever, the obsession of old. I needed a mind free and uncluttered, fixated upon nothing except the enemies from without.

How could I understand then how difficult this was? Psychologically, I was still confronted with the dreaded choice of yesteryear, and had very little sense of my own identity. I was now a man, but I had little emotional sense of who that man really was. Was I the cold, mental mechanic my father had seemed to be? Or was I the universal victim, the plaything of villains, mistreated, abused, that the madonna had so often seemed to be. I knew, even then, what I wanted to be, but how to cross the chasm, how to move across that floor to my father, while confronting the sad, piteous eyes of the madonna? I could not, even as an adult, bridge that chasm. Because I could not, the affair with Rosalie—and the despair which would later send me reeling toward a mental breakdown—was inevitable.

I met Rosalie in those last two months before graduation. Like Ruth, she too had the sorrowful, piteous eyes of the madonna, the expression of which bespoke pain and suffering. Unlike either of them, however, she had intellectual resources which helped her camouflage her true feelings, to present a bold and daring front to the world. As our relationship grew, I discovered that not only was she closely allied in actions and appearance to the madonna, but also that much of her history had been similar to mine. A Black woman, growing up in Harlem, attending an all-Black college, she too had known her Dorethas and Alexanders, had been shunned, abused, and cast aside because she was Black, not mulatto. Similarly, rejection for her had been almost as intense as it had been for me. I reflected, time and again during our walks together, that the ideas she related, those of the men who disparaged her, had also been mine, and I could not help but wander again, despite my newly found self-image, into self-laceration.

For how much had I contributed to her pain, despite the fact that I had known her for only two months? How much was I allied with those others, with even my past enemies like Alexander and Doretha, or the mulatto faculty at the school? Had I not also acted as they had, toward those like Rosalie, and did I not, now, owe restitution, not only for their sins, but for mine also? And what easier, cheaper way to make restitution, to absolve myself, than with Rosalie, who shared, it seemed, my need for solitude, whose moments of despair were almost as recurring as mine? All the easier, too, that she believed in things of the intellect, loving books filled with poetry, novels, plays. Once I attempted to break the relationship, one week before our graduation (she too was receiving a bachelor's degree); I manufactured a reason because I knew that she was moving too close, coming too near. After three days, however, I proposed to her, feeling that I would die without her. I implored her to come with me to California, to graduate school.

I thought little then of the new image I imagined that I reflected, not realizing that I was moving into the old pattern again, that I was seeing her not as a woman, but as an abstraction. I couldn't see that she was yet another Yvonne, to be saved this time not so much from the brutality of others, but from my own. I could not look at her without feeling my own pain reflected in her eyes, my rejection by the evil of the past, without wanting to prostrate myself before her. When I finally vaulted completely across the barricade of deception, able at last to see her as a human being, as a woman, I fled in panic, not so much because of her, but because of my own reflection, now revealed in the mirror of my psyche.

Had I not been so preoccupied with what I thought of then as my manifest destiny, I might have noticed the slight ruptures in our relationship during the year we spent in California. I was goading myself mercilessly toward achieving a master's degree. The successful completion of college, albeit at age thirty-three, like my completion of high school, had seemed, afterward, not the epitome of victory, but only the winning of a minor skirmish. I was gratified, to be sure, and my mother had even come to New York, at my insistence, to watch the ceremony. Afterward, I had sat alone until late in the morning, reliving the trials and tribulations, recreating the struggles of the past. But I remained unsatiated, unfulfilled. I wanted, needed still more successes.

Thus one day after receiving my bachelor's degree and a Jonas Salk Scholarship, I was overwhelmed by despair. This time, however, I could not disappear into isolation, for Rosalie and her presence were everywhere. I remember waking up in the morning mentally and emotionally fatigued, my heart racing as though propelled by a jet engine. Looking at the kind face buried beneath the pillow, I wondered when she would be gone, only to be jolted completely awake by the fact that she would not leave, that here was her home, that I was no longer alone.

And now I was struck by a sense of almost fearful desperation; I wanted to be alone, refused to be cheated out of these moments of sweet delirium by an intruder. I rushed from the bed, eased open drawers and clothes closets, confirming my worst fears: the evidence of Rosalie's presence was everywhere, in the kitchen, in the bathroom, the bedroom. I felt as if I were being strangled, stifled, with no place to retreat. How could I write, remain motionless, cry at whim, become almost catatonic?

I realized, finally, that I would have to suffer/enjoy my anguish in the presence of someone else, that I could not escape, as before, into myself.

The first week was as difficult for Rosalie as for me. The task of preparing for our trip to California fell upon her shoulders. Though I accompanied my mother to the bus station for her return home, I said little, and what little I did say, came mechanically, reflexively. My conversations with Rosalie were similarly automatic. We would sit at the dinner table, and she would be explaining something, in that staccato-like voice of hers, and I would be miles away, lost in a terrestrial fog, oblivious to all but the heavy sound of my own breathing.

The long train journey to California revived me somewhat, but I was immediately filled with an inexhaustible supply of nervous energy. I thought of the essays I wanted to write, of the coming course work, of the day when I would receive my master's degree, of going on for my doctorate. I dreamed of greater victories, of returning to Virginia one year later with the boast of two degrees, and—who knows?—perhaps articles, poems, or short stories published. The best years, I told myself, lay in the distance and what the past year's accomplishment had evidenced was the fact that I was capable of further successes. Yes, I thought of almost everything except the woman beside me, everything except my wife.

The first few months in California, she suffered near rejection, believing, as I suppose we both did, that my inattentiveness was due to the pressures of work. There were times, too, when I was very attentive, when we walked about the streets of dusty, hot Los Angeles, wandered amid the giant plants. I was tyrannized almost, it seemed, by the greenness of the city. The protest against the war in Vietnam had spread to the UCLA campus, and we attended rallies together, listened to the speeches, sat in on discussion groups. Such times, however, were rare. More often, I sat at my desk on days when school was not in session, from four in the morning until six at night, withdrawn, silent, preoccupied with work. Entire days were spent with other students, debating literature; and I just as frequently walked out at night into the empty spaces of Los Angeles, to be alone. These times, away from Rosalie, predominated.

After three months, the strain of her near isolation began to tell. I would awaken in the morning to her weeping, softly at first, then in time, more loudly. The sound of her anguished crying would bring me once again near despondency, almost immobilizing me, and I would be consumed with guilt and pity. I would then move to comfort her, to shower attention upon her, but when her crying stopped, my depression would linger. I would again feel threatened by her presence, craving isolation, and angry because I did not have it.

Three days before Christmas, the first of a series of similar scenes occurred. I had been at the library all day, having left her to do all the Christmas shopping. Rosalie had been crying before I arrived home, continued to do so after I had seated myself at my desk. For the first time she voiced her frustration, her anxieties: "I feel like I'm nothing. You're never here, and when you are, you might as well not be. I sit here all day looking at the walls, and even when you're here, I still look at the walls."

I had known that the explosion would come, gearing myself for it. Yet I did not know how to handle it. I tried to comfort her, to soothe her, to reason with her; she no longer accepted my entreaties, began only to cry, louder, harder. It was, I suppose, the intensity with which she cried, the energy, the pulsating, deafening roar of it, convulsing her body, which moved me for the first time not toward pity, but toward anger, almost to unbridled hatred. Those tears went back, I know now, to another time, to other tears, loud, hard. I quickly packed my few clothes, my books, my papers, and bounded into the cool Los Angeles night.

Outside, the anger subsided and the feelings of remorse began. How could I leave her and to what fate? And what would happen to me if I did leave her, what kind of retribution might I suffer? And what would happen to her, what kind of suffering would this woman undergo in such a strange, alien city? She would, eventually, I surmised, make her way back to New York; but what of the shame of facing her family? But more, I was convinced, as much as I could ever be convinced of such things, that she loved me, and what torture of spirit, what destruction of hope and faith would ensue upon my leaving? Yes, how much, I wondered, would she too suffer? I was overwhelmed, as before, with her pain: had I not been as guilty as those who had previously used her? I was in love with her, despite all, and if that were true, would not the experiences I was now undergoing benefit us both? Could I not make restitution to her and my father, as well as avenge myself on my enemies, by receiving a graduate degree and writing a novel? Beyond these questions, however, was the image of her I conjured up in my mind: abandoned, beaten, defeated, a pitiable woman, existing in tears and despair. I went back to the house, unpacked my suitcase, held her in my arms, was overwhelmed with mercy and tenderness. I did not know then how many times the experiences of that night would be repeated.

Our relationship improved somewhat during the second semester, when she enrolled at another college, the University of Southern California. Meanwhile, my first essay was published in the *Negro History Bulletin*, a critical piece, tracing the history of Black literature. I remember buying a bottle of wine to celebrate, of later buying up extra copies of the magazine, of sending them to family and friends, of autographing a copy for Rosalie. I had remained oblivious to much of the student activity on campus my first semester, and this continued during the second semester. Except for an occasional drink or two with a friend named Houston Baker, who helped me over a severe crisis during that first semester, or an occasional party, I devoted my time to work.

The friendship between Houston and me, which continues still, was based upon mutual respect, and was necessitated by the fact that we comprised only a handful of Black students in the UCLA graduate department. He was bright, argumentative, inquisitive—

and his knowledge of the literature complemented mine. I discovered in him an intellectual equal, and though we argued against each other, toward others, whites, we usually found ourselves, much to our mutual displeasure, on the same side of the argument. Houston was younger than I and from a different background. He had come to graduate school fresh from Howard University. During that first semester, when my grades had shrunk from an A— average to a B average, largely because of an altercation with, I believe even now, a racist professor, and my anxieties concerning my marriage, Houston had persuaded me to see the next semester through. I had done so and managed, by the end of the second semester, to score straight As, thus bringing my average back to what I considered respectability.

Our friendship survived despite my neglect of Rosalie, who occasionally commented upon the fact that I often ignored her for long hours of debate and argument with Houston. No friendship between myself and another man had survived until then, primarily, I know now, because the situation we had constructed so well resembled that which had once existed between my father and myself. The words flew between us, fast, furious, learned; we tackled the subject of "Paradise Lost," the imagery in the poetry of Keats, the importance of *Invisible Man*, the poetry in the prose of Baldwin. We read and commented upon each other's work, and after a debate with him—in which I always regarded myself as the superior—I would be close to manic drunkenness, exhilarated.

Armed with a master's degree, one published article, another already accepted for publication by *College Language Association Journal*, on the literature of Baldwin and Wright, Rosalie and I left Los Angeles in the summer of 1967. I was not to see Houston again for another five years, but I would remember our debates together. In later years, I would also recall, sadly, that outside of such experiences, I had known very little about Houston. His needs, his wants, his anxieties, his obsession remained unknown to me. It was not that he did not confide in me, that he did not reach across the threshold of our relationship to unburden himself of pain; only that I was as oblivious to his feelings as I was to Rosalie's, obsessed, as usual, with my own.

The usual elation, followed by despair, accompanied my achieving the master's degree and I postponed a planned trip to Virginia. Two degrees and two published articles were, to be sure, an accomplishment, but measured against what I hoped to accomplish, what my ego, buttressed by these two victories, assured me that I could accomplish, they were not yet enough for me to return to the town. We returned directly to New York instead, and with the assistance of Leslie Berger, whom I had met earlier in undergraduate school at CCNY, I received a position as lecturer in the English department of the school from which I had graduated some fifteen months before.

A small band of us appointed at that time, including some who had been appointed earlier, were members of the English department in name only. We had actually been hired to teach in the SEEK program, one of the positive results of the revolt of the sixties, a program which Leslie Berger and his colleague Bernard Levy had instituted, above the objections of the general faculty. These objections had been based on racial grounds. The program, originally called the Pre-Baccalaureate Program, had been designed to allow more Blacks and Puerto Ricans to attend college, CCNY, situated in an area adjacent to the neighborhoods in which many of them lived. It called for waiving of the unusually high average which kept all but a minority of such students out of the college, by basing admission on other educational criteria. The route for most Black and Puerto Rican students had been previously that which I had followed: non-matriculated status during the evening hours, until at least a B average was achieved, whereupon the student was awarded matriculated status. Thus CCNY had managed over the years to remain 99 per cent white in terms of both faculty and student body.

Because I and my few colleagues, including Toni Cade and Barbara Christian (later to establish themselves in the field of writing), were hired specifically to teach these youngsters, we were regarded as pariahs not only by the general faculty, but by the English department to which we were assigned. We were given no office space, barred from serving on department committees, segregated at one far end of the campus. We had our own director, appointed by the chairman of the English department, who served as the middleman between us and a hostile department.

The attitudes of the department regarding the young students and their teachers, extended to almost every Black or Puerto Rican. This attitude was evidenced when, in the spring of 1968, my second semester, I decided to alter my curriculum, choosing books other than those suggested by the director. The results of that skirmish were later recorded in the essay "Not So Soon One Morning," which I published shortly thereafter. I had announced my intentions to supplement the existing texts—an anthology of essays compiled by the chairman of the department and one of his collegues, and two novels, *The Catcher in the Rye*, and *A Portrait of the Artist*—with an anthology of Black literature, *Soon One Morning*, compiled by Herbert Hill, and *Down These Mean Streets*, the award-winning book by Piri Thomas. I had not wanted to eliminate the other books, had not sought to use only Black and Puerto Rican material—all of my intellectual training, from my father onward argued then, as now, against such segregation of ideas—but only to integrate this material with the other. The proposal was denounced by the director, commented upon derisively by other members of the department, argued vigorously in our small group, with the Black teachers supporting my position.

With such support and my insistent threats that I would resign and make an issue of the affair, the two books I had demanded were included in my curriculum. Other Black teachers would later do the same, and the white teachers in our group would also follow suit. I was surprised at the hostility toward the inclusion of Black and Puerto Rican literature, if only because the courses were segregated, consisting of 99 per cent Blacks and Puerto Ricans. It was not white students, therefore, whom I wanted to teach the literature, but students whom I knew would receive nothing of Black literature were they lucky enough to move on to English classes in the general college.

My own experience on that score served as a reminder. I had moved, during the sixties and the great wave of white liberalism, from college through graduate school as an English literature major, had been assigned close to five hundred books, not one of which had been written by a Black writer. Both in undergraduate school and in graduate school, whenever a term paper was required with projects concerning authors outside the course material permitted, I had chosen a project based upon a Black writer. This choice was invariably met with silent disdain and later grudging acceptance of the project. The most meaningful of such experiences occurred at UCLA, in a class devoted to twentieth-century literature. Our term paper assignment was a broad one—we might choose any twentieth-century writer approved by the professor.

The writer must have written more than one book and have had enough critical attention paid to his work to warrant at least ten critical articles about it. Based on my previous experiences at City College, I had expected the usual resistance to my project—an analysis of the writings of James Baldwin, and when I had gone to see the advisor, I remember announcing my intention determinedly.

He had paused, waved a cigar in the air, swung around in his swivel chair: "Well . . . I think that Baldwin is a great essayist . . . a great essayist . . . but a novelist . . . ?" He looked from me to the ceiling. I said nothing. I had not come to argue.

He placed the cigar in a glass ashtray, smiled at me: "Of course, the authors we're reading, as you know, are people like Mann, Camus, Dostoevski, Malraux . . ."

I could not resist a sarcastic rejoinder: "We're also reading Bellow, Mailer, Roth . . ." My voice trailed off.

The smile in his face turned to a smirk. He picked up the cigar again, then chuckled to himself. "I see your intended point . . . but . . . well . . . fine . . . let's see what you can find out about Baldwin . . . but remember . . ."—the smirk returned to his face —"you need at least ten critical articles."

I was not expected to find them, despite the fact that Baldwin was the most talked-about Black writer of the sixties. I discovered more than ten articles in the Black magazines alone; and I discovered articles by Black writers about Black writers and Black writing, material stretching back to the 1920s. Much of this material was to be included in *Black Expression*, my first anthology, and the first of its kind in America to be devoted to Black criticism alone.

Despite my heavy teaching load—those of us in the Prebac program taught four days—the teachers in the English department, three—I began to write and publish feverishly. The antagonisms between Rosalie and myself had been somewhat mitigated by our return to New York, though there were still many anxiety-filled moments. Still, Rosalie helped me prepare material for publication, sometimes helping me to clarify my own ideas by suggesting her own.

Two years after returning to New York, I had published over thirty articles, one short story, and had edited an anthology, soon to be released. I was under contract to two publishers, Doubleday and Horizon Press, was feted at lunches and dinners by at least three others. Though I wrote occasional pieces for white magazines, most of my work was published in Black magazines, in *Black World* and *Liberator Magazine*, both of whose editors became lasting good friends. Though I was still plagued by bouts of despair, I ventured, sporadically, outside of my isolation to take part in Black Power conferences, to attend book parties, poetry readings. I met men and women who would remain lifelong acquaintances, Don L. Lee, Hoyt Fuller, Imamu Baraka, John Killens, Gwendolyn Brooks, John Williams, John Henrik Clarke.

In the summer of 1969, when Horizon Press scheduled the release of *The Black Situation*, a collection of personal essays, I was engulfed by waves of manic elation. Together, Rosalie and I made plans for a trip to Paris, while we dined at some of the restaurants which editors and publishers had introduced me to. For a week following receipt of the crisp, freshly printed author's copies of *Black Expression*, we experienced a oneness, a togetherness lacking since the beginning of our marriage, now three years ago.

The hunger of old had been somewhat satiated and I knew now that I was ready to return to Virginia, ready to bask in the triumph so long coming. I had finally downed my adversaries, proven them wrong. At thirty-seven I had finally evened the scorecard which I had carried around in my breast during most of those years. And the future held evidence of more triumphs to come. I had already completed two other books, a biography of Paul Laurence Dunbar, later entitled *Oak and Ivy*, and an anthology, *Bondage, Freedom and Beyond*. Meanwhile, I had begun collecting a group of essays based upon the theme of the Black Aesthetic. My essays on literature and social events had brought me enemies, newer ones, whom I welcomed because they could be dealt with on intellectual grounds. They were primarily whites—critics and social commentators on Black literature and life—whom I had purposely, selectively, set out to attack. Essays were, as I saw them, weapons, more immediate and direct than fiction, and, perhaps, still smarting under my guilt from being absent from the Black struggle during most of the sixties, I surrendered the ambition to write fiction and dedicated myself to non-fiction prose, successfully joining others to wage warfare against white arrogance and hypocrisy.

As for that other war, however—more severe, longer lasting—

between myself and the past, I was, I believed then, winning decisively, now able to brandish symbols of conquest, affluence, recognition of a sort, notation and references secured in books and scholarly journals. Such symbols were not only proof of success, but the fruits of it, and in manic delirium for long periods of time, I gathered them as fruit, wolfed them down, voraciously, gluttoned myself upon them. Then suddenly, three months after publication of *Black Expression*, I was to chase and capture one of the most prized symbols of all and, almost immediately afterward, be hurled back into despair, jolted into it to such a degree that I was not to re-emerge whole again until five years later.

The incident involved Brooks Brothers department store! Years back, during my first weeks in New York, I had wandered downtown, around the Madison Avenue vicinity; peering into the store window, I had caught glimpses of the men and women entering the store—neatly dressed, white, striding confidently, purposely through the oaken doors. Standing in my worn khaki pants and run-down loafers, I had envied them, tried to shield myself from their eyes. I hadn't wanted them to notice that I stood drooling over the long white terry cloth bathrobe on display in the window, hadn't wanted them to know that I fantasized wrapping myself up in it, losing myself in it. Finally, I had moved away from the window, almost fleeing back to the subway train bound for Harlem.

As Rosalie and I pushed through the heavy oaken doors, on this occasion, the very act of entering seemed intimidating, for the doors did not give way to a light, timid push. On the transom above the door, etched in gold lettering beneath a sign of the Golden Fleece, the store's emblem, were the words "Founded: 1880." Inside, the decor consisted of evenly spaced rows of display cases, garnished oaken walls, neatly dressed casually stationed salesmen striking a number of poses near the display cases exhibiting hand-tailored shirts, cashmere sweaters, ties woven from expensive cloth, terry cloth and seersucker bathrobes; farther off were displayed shoes of expensively tanned leather. Suddenly my credits—my articles, my books, my position—seemed inconsequential, and I was back to my early days in Harlem, where to walk into a downtown department store was to be scrutinized suspiciously by the store's personnel. I found myself, shortly after entering Brooks Brothers, glancing in anticipation from one salesman to another. I speculated on which was the store detective: Maybe the one in the single-breasted suit, looking in our direction, or maybe the one beside the elevator in the candy-striped tie. I wanted to know which one he was. I wanted him to see my hands. I wanted him to know that I had not stolen anything. Yet how could I tell which one was the detective? They were all, I thought, looking at me, watching me, waiting for me to steal something.

Not only the salesman and the store detective, whoever he was, but the customers also seemed to stare. The blond woman with the man in the tweed suit, she was looking at me; so too was the man spraying cologne on his arm, so too the man trying on shoes in the rear and the small boy fingering the cardigan sweater—all were watching me out of the corners of their eyes, thinking the same thoughts, asking the same question: What is he doing here? And each, I believed, arrived at the same answer: To steal! What else? *Yes, what else. If not that, then he shouldn't be here, has no right to be here. And he knows it too. Look at him trembling; look at him perspiring; see the awkward way he leans when he talks to the salesman.*

And listen to him speak: who ever heard a nigger talk like that? Look at him walk toward the elevator, trying to walk stiffly, head up in the air—he is almost tripping over his own feet. No, he does not belong here.

Once on the second floor, where the suits and sport coats were, I nervously slid in and out of jackets, mindful of the eyes of the salesman, who was immaculate in a double-breasted suit.

"It looks nice," Rosalie said, appraising the brown tweed jacket.

I remembered Alice's father, the tweed jacket which had become, for me, his trademark, made of conservative, rich-looking fabric. I smiled, even through my anxiety, gloating inwardly at the fact that mine was more expensive-looking, the fabric of a better quality, than his ever had been. "I think I'll take it," I said to the salesman.

He smiled, asked nonchalantly, "Will that be cash or charge, sir?"

"Why . . . cash!" I blurted out quickly. Charge? Me? A charge account here? Why, I wondered, was he asking me this? Did he think that he had to be nice? Why the damn condescension?

He took my measurements, folded the jacket, chalk-marked

some pants I had bought, hung them on a hanger, said, matter-of-factly, "Why don't you open a charge account?"

I glanced at Rosalie, who stood seemingly unperturbed. "Why don't you?" she asked.

I turned reluctantly to the salesman, heard myself asking, "Why don't I? What do I do?"

"Nothing. We'll send you a bill with the suit; then you will have established a charge account."

"What?" I expounded, incredulously.

He laughed. "That's all there is to it. Really."

I remember the ride back down in the elevator, remember that I was no longer perspiring, that I did not, now, glance nervously about me, that I swaggered somewhat, a commanding tone coming to my voice, remember the forceful, bouncing stride toward the counter containing the spotless white terry cloth bathrobes. I felt elated, manic, proud, arrogant, secure, safe. I had opened a charge account at Brooks Brothers. After that, the deluge.

They were all mine now, these symbols of success which I had longed so much to expropriate. I had acquired all that I believed necessary to erase my ugly image, to make people notice things about me other than my black skin, my kinky hair, my thick lips. Those who had so shamed me in Virginia were now, I felt, no longer my superiors, no longer ordained by custom and tradition to violate my sense of humanity. The boyhood dreams of vengeance and recrimination had become real; I had been transformed, miraculously, into a darker replica of Alice's father and Alexander, no longer needing to cower before their image. I had thwarted the prophecy of those who had predicted for me a bad end, and could return now, not in disgrace but in honor, willing to measure my accomplishments against those of the sons and daughters of Newport News's middle class. As for this white America, I recalled the lines from Baldwin: "This country sat you down in the ghetto to die." But I had not died. Their laws and their hostility, their calculated designs to break my spirit had failed. I had overcome them too, had persevered, had endured.

Still, three days after the visit to Brooks Brothers, alone with my thoughts and my typewriter, waves of remorse, and then despair, swept down upon me, and I remember suddenly feeling very tired and very sad, very old and somewhat angered. I remember calling my mother's name, whispering something intelligible, I thought, to my father, and being overwhelmed by the tremendous need to sleep and to cry. It was almost as if I were coming apart from myself, then being rejoined to myself, and though I did not, that time, lose consciousness, I fought back wave after wave of darkness by pounding on my typewriter. Either then or later during the night—I discovered the next morning—I had written part of a soliloquy: "But, Lucifer, I want to hear the true story. I want the legend as it really happened, the way I see it in my own mind. I want to know whether or not your revolution really failed, or whether, as I believed, you really did best him, dethrone him. Did you also become him? And by so doing did you not then, in horror and revulsion, come to see what his heaven really was: the refugee of the tyrant, miscreant, bigot, sycophant, ass-kisser, antihumanist, hypocrite? And when the great revelation came, did you not voluntarily then become, as the poet was to describe you, the outsider, the exile, the fallen angel?"

I returned home to Virginia in the spring of 1970, during the Easter week vacation, less in triumph than in despair. The bouts with despondency came frequently now, leaving me teary for long stretches of time. I could manage few manic highs, even when *The Black Situation* was released or when I received an appointment as Assistant Professor of English at Bernard Baruch College of the City University of New York. I managed, however, to move through my work schedule even more vigorously, meeting new people professionally, addressing college audiences, writing a critical study of Claude McKay for Broadside Press, a Black publishing company. I maintained a quiet composure for those whom I met—for a few hours, at work, in business meetings. The years of having camouflaged my feelings now served me well, but with Rosalie, this was impossible. She saw me in my worst moments, discerned that something was wrong but did not know what. Once again, she grew increasingly distressed by my isolation. Gradually, as in California, her frustration and hostility grew, reaching the point of explosion. "Look!" she shouted angrily one Sunday evening, three weeks before our trip to Virginia. "You don't see me . . . it's like I'm some kind of abstraction. But I'm your wife . . . your wife."

I was sitting at my desk, reading the proofs of *The Black Aesthetic* as I had for most of the day, pausing only to sleep or eat. It was not the harsh, accusing sound of her voice that caused me to react convulsively, that sent blood pounding to my head. She had not only invaded my isolation, but she had uttered too that word, "wife," which gave her the right to speak, which meant that she would continue to question me—not only now, but forever. The fears of women I had known slid like ghosts from the past, and I arose from the desk, bounded past her and through the door in panic. I was afraid, but unable to tell her why. How could she have understood, even if I had been able to explain my fears? How could I tell her that to be a husband meant belonging to someone, inviting the possibility, perhaps the probability, of rejection? How could she know that I had long ago assured myself that I would never risk that? To risk rejection was to risk all.

Outside, I moved through the Harlem streets toward the East River, a shadow merging with other shadows. I climbed the bridge linking Manhattan and the Bronx, and peering down into the murky water, wondering what it would be like if I were to jump, "to cease," I remembered the lines from Keats, "upon the midnight with no pain."

I saw Rosalie, the piteous victim of my imagination, her face wet with tears. Even above the soft murmur of the waves, I imagined her voice shrieking. As before, I was torn between love and hate, wanting to run away from the tears as much as I wanted to still the chaos to bring back the peace, to put my arms about her and kiss away those tears. Much later, when the sun had begun to emerge through the clouds of darkness, I had returned home to find Rosalie asleep, a book still open, head resting on the pillow.

We traveled to Virginia together, each of us bearing our own terrible emotional burden, the tension between us still raging. The city exacerbated those tensions. For me, the age-old longing, the many fantasized scenarios of triumph turned out to be little more than romantic dreams, conjured up by my ever fertile imagination. Whereas I had seen myself returning in elation, confronting the enemies of old, bestowing my presents and accomplishments upon the well-wishers of the past, I was now unwilling to confront my enemies at all, no longer desiring to force their acceptance. I visited only those few teachers who had been kind to me, giving them copies of my books. I avoided Alice's father, Alexander, Doretha, the others. Even while talking to those who had been kind to me, I was filled with a strange sense of guilt, of shame, unable to muster self-assurance.

Those whom I encountered on the streets, my old antagonists, were now old and doting, their stance no longer threatening and terrifying. I felt no anger for them, only an intense pity. I met acquaintances from my high school days, those who had gone to the shipyard, or who spent their days working the white folk's kitchen, old, beaten, these young men and women seemed dead and beaten long before their time, their lives ended at ages so very young. I scouted the area where the pimps and prostitutes had once plied their trade, books in hand, searching for Tillie and Red Drag. They were nowhere to be found, and to the new generation of pimps and prostitutes, they were unknown. Some of these new ones had also been high school acquaintances, but they were of a different time, were indeed a new breed. Their eyes held none of the kindness of the pimps and prostitutes of yesteryear; their conversations toward outsiders were snarling, harsh, hostile. Their threatening bodies smelled like those who had been swallowed up by the shipyard, like the ancient dead.

There were others, too, whom I had once known who now seemed the deadest of the dead. Unable to face the slow death of the shipyard or that of the street, they stood nodding, zombielike in hallways, against the sides of buildings which had once held children who had never heard of such things as "horse" or "smack." Their death was caused by others, who cruised the streets in long, sleek limousines, or walked about in gaudy, expensive clothes. They were shifty-eyed men, the selfishness evident in their carriage, the disdain for the walking dead visible in their manner.

I found myself empathizing with all of them, questioning the whys and wherefores of their destiny as opposed to mine, and I became saddened at the disparity between us, almost pained that I was among the living, had escaped their fate. But the awful reality of their existence bounded into my consciousness, I might well have shared their fate, might still share it. No matter what I had told myself, the millennium had not truly been reached, the protective armor with which I had sought to enclothe myself was still filled with holes. I was still Black, and thus could never know what act of white men, what calamity would hurl me from the precipice, thrust me among the breathing dead. Other calamities, like that which had struck my father, leaving him suddenly little more than a vegetable, natural calamities, over which one had little control, were just as fearful. Kings could be transformed into something worse than beggars, almost instantaneously.

I came to avoid the streets, spending time instead with rela-tives: my aunts, my grandmother, my sisters, the madonna. After the initial conversational greetings were over, they demanded little of me, allowing me to sit staring off into space as they talked. Rosalie, however, was not among them, and she could not take either my inattentiveness, or my short, mechanical responses to questions I had not heard. On one occasion, Rosalie fled from the kitchen to our bedroom, to throw herself upon the bed, weeping the tears of the lonely and the rejected.

This time, I could not move to comfort her, did not even want to do so. My mind was too clouded, and too nagged with visions of the lifeless, with questions concerning my successful achievements. Was I really a good writer possessing talent, or was I a fluke, brought into being by the Black Power movement, which caused publishers and editors to acquire Black writers, as pimps acquired women for their stables? Did I deserve my professorship at the university or was this too a gift of the white people, an act of their condescension? I could not answer such questions, and that fact only intensified my fears, adding weight to my anguish.

If the visit to Virginia had exacerbated the state of depression in which I now found myself mired, the trip to Paris, later that summer, was the catalyst to push me across the emotional brink between despair and depression. Even as we stepped off the plane at Orly Airport, on our way to a hotel on the Left Bank, the war between Rosalie and me waged on. I had wanted to postpone the trip or, better still, to take one alone, but had acceded to her wishes, hoping, too, that the romantic trip might prevent the inevitable separation or divorce between us.

How could we have imagined, even then, that exactly the reverse would occur? Certainly those first few days, due, I suppose, to a different environment, brightened me up, offering no evidence of the rupture yet to come. Together we enjoyed the parks and gardens, making the cafes and Paris streets our playground. We were epicureans who, despite our anguished and tension-filled moments, found time to drink wine and make love and laugh, trying to inoculate ourselves against the eternal sickness. I still remember those days and hours of walking across the Seine, over to the Right Bank, down past the Louvre, into the garden of the Tuileries.

I remember, fondly, walking one bright midday the length of the Tuileries, moving up from the Louvre and down to the Champs Élysées. We had paused to watch the children sailing boats in the ponds, the tourists wide-eyed and happy, the old men and women playing *boules* on the rich green grass. I also remember the lumpy hotel bed and the ambitious clerk, who tried with no success to book us—two walkers—on the endless tours of the city—including one to the Louvre, just three blocks from our residence.

There are memories, too, of the both of us daring the French traffic, poking our tongues out at the speeding little cars as they disappeared down the narrow streets. We made treks up and down the enormous boulevards, St. Germain, St. Marcel, Du Montparnasse—through the Algerian quarter, the quarter of the saints, going in and out of the sidewalk cafes, the parks, laughing along with the people who laughed at the man with the dancing bear. There was also the trip to Versailles, I remember. With the crowds of tourists, we saw the magnificent halls of Louis XIV and his once private eden—forests and geometric gardens, a lake shaped like a parabola, surrounded by plush greens and yellows and browns. It was a setting defying superlatives, almost beyond description.

Most of all, though, I remember the trip to Chartres, the cathedral of which Baldwin had once written so eloquently. We had sat in awe in the silence and solemnity of its interior, as men and women, hooded priests and nuns, walked slowly through the halls of this centuries-old monument. And I remember, too, that the despair sprang full again then and I became saddened, almost as silent and transfixed as the figurines adorning the aged walls. Even as I sat there, awed by the beauty and splendor of it all, I knew that our marriage could not last, that all human relationships were destined to end, as I had long believed.

"Was it realistic, Rosalie," I was to ask in my journal years later, "for us to ask for, expect an extension of time?" Our one week in Paris had eased some of the tension, recapturing what had, in sporadic moments, once been. What right did we have to ask for more? Why did we not realize that this uncounted assortment of minutes and hours was, for us, the whole of eternity, that they would last, in our minds, as long as the monuments? They would survive the years with an energy, a freshness, a vibrancy not equaled even by the monuments. We knew none of this then, would not know it on our return to America. After the romanticism and togetherness of Paris, we would become warriors again, our days and nights filled with mutual recriminations, with hostility. In desperation, I would announce, painfully, that I would leave, would repeat the phrase time and time again, until soon the decision was so much a part of my consciousness that I had no other choice.

Having made the decision, however, and communicated it to Rosalie, I was beset by new waves of despair, of panic and fear. I had brought the tears of yesterday once again to her eyes, was duplicating the actions of others in her past. Moreover, for something so ephemeral, I thought, as isolation, I was committing an act against her similar to that committed against the madonna. I was thrusting Rosalie aside, leaving her, so I imagined, among the breathless dead. I sought other options, prolonging the agony for both of us, making more frequent trips to the Manhattan Bridge, where I stared even more longingly into the dirty waters of the East River, hearing again and with greater intensity the lines from the Keats poem.

I thought often of suicide in those weeks, and only the welcome pressure of work managed, I believe, to pull me back again and again from the brink. I had signed a three-book contract with Doubleday, had begun research on the first book, a history of the Black novel. With my promotion to Associate Professor of English at Baruch College, I was visiting, almost every other week, a college to deliver or take part in a seminar. I managed all of these things and more, despite the inner turmoil—or perhaps because of it—managing to allow my friends to see me only in safe, secure moments. By the spring of 1971, however, the pressures of having vacillated over the decision for over six months, forced me to act, irrevocably. Still, I could not leave until three months later—and the need for alienation brought on by the final decision drove me to accept an old offer, to become visiting Professor of English at the University of Washington in Seattle.

I left Kennedy Airport on the morning of June 7, 1971, just five days after my thirty-ninth birthday; the lines of worry and anxiety creased my face. I had not slept more than four hours a night for four months, and my movements were jerky, spasmodic, restless.

My eyes seemed to tear easily, and my appetite, since my return from Paris, was almost non-existent—I ate scarcely more than one meal a day. A new city, I hoped, would give me time for pause, for recollection, for much needed rest. Rosalie had accompanied me to the airport and once aboard the plane, my eyes had over-flowed as I recalled her admonition to me to rethink my decision to leave, upon my return. "Give me another chance," she had said plaintively, "let's try again, perhaps it will work out."

The words remained etched upon my mind, like the tears which disappeared and reappeared, blinding me to the sights far below, made me oblivious to time. I do not know, therefore, when, following the direction of the stewardess, I looked out of the aircraft from my window on the right, half rose in my seat, al-most upsetting the glass of wine which had succored me, as the giant mountain Rainier came suddenly, magnificently into view. Here, over ten thousand feet above the earth, this white-clad mountain stood out from all the others, in superb majesty, in confident isolation, unperturbed, even by the snowstorm that raged in the beginning of summer about its peaks.

I had seen mountains before, would see them again in far dis-tant places, would always be, as then, awed by their presence. But Rainier would remain for me, prince among them all, a symbol for the lonely, the defeated, for those who sought security in de-tachment, peace in isolation, grace in alienation. It suggested to me, now so devoid of the old fire, that the volcano within, though contained, still lived, that the reservoir of passion and feeling was not dried up. Temporarily, I was able to put my despairing specu-lations toward the back of my mind, and by the time David picked me up at the airport, my thoughts had shifted from myself to the magnificent mountain in the distance.

Throughout our ride from the airport to my apartment, secured by the university, to David's obvious discomfort, I talked about Rainier, learned that he had visited the mountain several times; he reminded me of a fact I had forgotten, that the mountain had been given considerable mention in the novel *Let Me Breathe Thunder*, by the black writer William Attaway. Gradually, our conversation shifted to other things, to mutual friends, to his posi-tion at the university, but we both knew that Rainier continued to occupy my attention. Later that night, the mountain clouded, hidden from view by the darkness, my personal difficulties came back to my mind and I begged off having dinner with David and his wife to sit, to think, alone.

David Lorrens was Assistant Professor of English at the university and director of its Black Studies Program. Younger than I by some seven years, he too was a writer, a gifted poet and essayist. We had conversed before, had read each other's works, had even communicated by letter, when I had asked him for an article to be included in the anthology *The Black Aesthetic*, but we had never met before. We discovered, however, that we were emotionally, intellectually, and ideologically compatible, and during my stay, we met almost daily, until soon conversations which had begun by reference to the Black situation in America, moved to encompass those which dealt with the very personal. He was, for the most part, a quiet man, detached, somewhat like myself, and in his breast too, I was to discover, much later, beat the drums of despair and despondency. I told him of the depression of the past, of that which still afflicted me daily, of the impending separation from Rosalie, of the fears, more pronounced in these last few days, that the talent I had once possessed, that which had enabled me to write like one in a frenzy, had been burned to cinders. I told him that I doubted if I were capable of completing work on the history of the Black novel, that I doubted, even, if I would ever be able to write again.

He would listen calmly, hands held close to his side, as we walked down the narrow tree-lined streets decorated by little shops and stores which served the college community, to reappear on other streets filled with roomy houses, surrounded by bouquets of red, green, pink flowers and giant bushes of ferns, their greenness accentuated in the misty fog, all dwarfed by the giant, ever white peaks of Rainier, looming statuesque, ominously in the distance.

He would offer careful advice, guarded, point out some contradiction in my logic, through kindness, but most of all by listening, he attempted to console me, to inspire me, to inject me with renewed confidence. Only when I spoke of suicide, did his voice raise, did he become passionate, argue with me instead of reasoning with me. Had I not been so preoccupied with my own problems, had my own emotional dearth not prevented me from being able to decipher coded messages from another troubled soul, I might have understood that our daily conversations were as therapeutic for him as for me, that he too needed someone who might help him breach the barricades of his own feelings, some-one less preoccupied with himself than I, who might have laid the foundation, then, for preventing the catastrophe, but one year in the future, which would overwhelm him and drive him to suicide.

I discovered in him, however, in his wife and brother, willing ears, confidants who drew me into their orbit, despite my insist-ence on isolation, on alienation, who seemed to realize that seclu-sion was part of my character, even my strength, and who did not attempt to emotionally possess me, did not demand that I be-come emotionally clean before them, did not, like a pickpocket, attempt to rummage through the secret chambers of my psyche. The students also played their part in helping me, not to rid my-self of despondency, but to mitigate its effect, by offering their warmth, their gaiety, their innocence, by being willing to accept me as I was. I moved, therefore, toward some kind of emotional stability, began to laugh, infrequently again, to rest better, to drink the cheap wines the students suggested, to feel better about myself and even to contemplate the coming separation with less of a sense of dread. I began to relish the early morning walks about the city, alone, to feel more confident, to arise, early in the morning before dawn to write. I made frequent calls to Rosalie, and though often times jolted back into despair by the sobbing and weeping which swept across vast spaces to assault my mind, my psyche, I managed to avoid slipping into total despair. It was at this point, six weeks after my arrival, that I made the pilgrim-age to Rainier.

My romantic attraction to the mountain had driven me earlier to the university library, to *Let Me Breathe Thunder*, and I had learned that "Nisqually," the greatest of gods, according to the In-dian legend, created the earth and everything in it. Afterward, the god had nothing left to do. He became an obstacle to his own creations, for he was outside of every pattern that he had made. In a desperate attempt to find some niche for himself, some iden-tity even, he roamed the state of Washington, his giant footprints leaving valleys, caverns, mountains in his wake. In this way the Cascades, the conglomeration of miniature mountains surround-ing the great white mountain, had been formed. Later, he himself squatted down "among the Cascades and [became] a mountain—a terrible smoking mountain for ages—Rainier. . . . The old God stayed put after a fashion . . . but the Indians say that his tormented spirit still moans and moans, and in its misery sometimes breathes thunder."

Having left David, his wife, and the small group of students who had accompanied us to the mountain, I had walked off alone, stood looking up at the snow white peaks and down at the Cascades below, at the gray-green rocks drenched by water trickling down from the melting snow. With what awe and condescension, I wondered, had the first Indian looked upon this mountain? Did he notice that the volcano, though quiet (was it quiet then, also?) seemed still alive, that the thunder, though muted, seemed as vociferous as ever? Did he feel something of his own mortality, his own insignificance, his own powerlessness; but did he feel too an exuberance of spirit, a renewed faith in himself, new inspiration?

Down below, way below, was the vibrant pulsating world, with all its excitement and terror, where tormented men roamed the streets, moving within patterns, without pause, without reflection. Here, on the other hand, time was capsulized, embalmed, motion paralyzed; there were no patterns save those made by the still wet snow and the angular designs of the Cascades. There was awe here, but no terror, and the noise was not of rushing men, but of one's own thoughts. The words of the old spiritual came to my mind, "I went to the rock to hide my face, but the rock cried out no hiding place." There was here, however, a hiding place, not for all time, no, not that, but for a while, momentarily, where, in reflection upon this silent strength, one might refuel his own, and in time need no hiding place anywhere.

For the great white mountain, towering grotesquely among the smaller Cascades, dwarfed everything in its surroundings, was, surely, outside of all patterns, seemed to fit nowhere, to have no place. Still, despite this, it stood magnificent, undaunted, proud and fearsome, the maker of legends, the inspirer of poets, the object of romance. Now, suddenly, I was caught up in the romantic dream, felt exhilarated, manic, hungered for my pen and paper, for my typewriter; I wanted to write of this mountain, of its beauty, its poise; I wanted to compose a hymn to it, write a poem to it. But beyond that, I wanted too, to write a hymn to myself, a poem to myself. I wanted to stare down all the mysteries of my past, look back through the years, as I now looked out and beyond the snow-capped peaks, wanted to move, like "Nisqually," through the Cascades of my own mind, wanted to unleash the volcano within.

What I had understood then, something to which I would be able to give words only after my sessions with Raphael, was that despite my insistence to the contrary, I had not been able, myself, to formulate patterns of my own choosing—I had always lived, even during those rebellious times, by those of others. I had been afraid not to, afraid to risk the dangers of being different, not ready to accept isolation on any but my own terms. I had sought safety and security, even though I knew that such were in white America ephemeral at best. I had sought to emulate other men, to capture their images, to surrender my identity to them, believing that not to do so meant to face disaster. No, I had not chosen isolation, but had been forced into it, had not really wanted it, desired it, but had been comfortable with it, because it protected me from the outside, left me alone with myself, shielded me from the chaos and tumult of living. But I did not need my analyst in order to understand three months later, Rainier and Seattle behind me, as I stood, bags packed, saying my last good-bys to Rosalie, that I was following still another pattern, that I had at last made the choice that I could not make yesteryear; that I had become one with the old desired image.

And so I stood, living tom-toms in my head. Whirlpools deep, so deep in my stomach, I was a historical animal. I was a reincarnation of what was. I was him and me, father and child, asking the questions of old, wanting an answer, fearing an answer, now living the answer—all of it; the sad piteous words, mirrored in tear-filled eyes, as Rosalie tried to muster the courage after having cried for so long never to cry again, trying in this climactic moment to hold fast, not to falter, to confront the inevitable bravely, with dignity. And she stared at me with ancient eyes and it was I who withered, almost sank, felt the whirlpools deep inside now, heard the toms-toms growing louder, pushing crescendo-like against the pit of my skull. And I began, instinctively, to sense something of what it was like then at that time, began to understand in some small way that little of it had anything to do with his love for the madonna or for me, that sometimes men stepped outside of their particular histories for reasons which they could not comprehend, running not so much from love, but from themselves, not because they wanted to, but because they had to.

And we both had to. Father and son. Terrified men—frightened men. Afraid to dare the unknown, and thus leaving ruin in our paths, monuments not so much to our cruelty, but to our depression. We were haters who, despite all, could not hate, pragmatists who could never down the romantic within, poets who lived always close to the tragic. And how much, I realized, had I not understood. *For all my life, old man, I hated and loved you, fought against you, yes, you and many surrogates, molded the hot hatred into a moving ball of fire, tried to scorch everything that reminded me of you, tried to undermine what you were, even in those times—especially those times—when I wrote so eloquently and movingly about you—in those essays when you stand out as a kind of eighteenth-century hero and, though hero you are, it is always I who vanquish you, who emerge victorious, and even in your dying, yes, even there, it is I who remain victorious, yes, for no matter that afterward I might try to cover it up, rationalize it in print, even then, while sitting at your graveside, I did not cry for you, would not let myself cry for you, was not truly sorry that you were dead, because I would no longer be able to humiliate you by becoming something that you did not want me to become; and all those years of raw naked hatred, the terrors, fears, spent in hating you, in fleeing from you were in vain, yes, because now I know and I cannot tell Rosalie—no more than you could tell me—cannot find the words to still the hurt, the pain, to hold back the coming years of despair and anguish, cannot say that I leave, Rosalie, not because I do not love you—for love you I do, yes, so very much, but I leave because I must. I love you, but I must go!*

We separated in August of 1971, and after a brief trip to Paris to lecture at the Sorbonne, I returned to New York, to take up residence in Westchester. Yet I came back often to stand looking up into her window. Sometimes there were lights and I imagined that I saw her face, those sad eyes behind big bifocals—a sensitive, beautiful, Black face that sometimes laughed and smiled, now laughing and smiling no longer. Does she, I wondered, sit and cry and think of better times? Does she hate me very much? Would she believe that I too suffer, am pained? Does she know that I dream nightly of her, awake, sometimes, terrified at the sound of her voice in my ears? Does she know that I write now, sometimes, fifteen, twenty pages a day in order to still the voice, to ease the pain.

Why should she be wiser than I was? I never discerned my father's anguish or his pain. I did not know if, sometimes, he too came in the darkness, in the peace of night, to sit and wonder what I might be doing behind closed doors, if he thought of me then, wanted to touch me, to reach out to me, to say, "The poet was wrong; it is not so much hope that dwells in the human breast, but love and it is possible, yes, despite all of this. It is possible if we are strong enough and brave enough and if we dare enough; for when disaster comes, we have nothing else, nothing but the love we have had and must have . . ." And the thought came, too, deep from the despair within, that if he had loved me, so too did the madonna. Yes, even when *they* possessed her, made her theirs, deprived me of her, she must have loved me too, but was unable to demonstrate it in any way, outside of buying me presents, enduring punishment from them, for me. Perhaps she didn't know in her simple way that an embrace, a kiss, a fond hand laid alongside an equally fond one, said that I love you far better than presents, than anything . . .

I would return from the house Rosalie and I once shared, late in the morning, return to dress for work, or, on those days when there was no school, to my typewriter. Work became my bulwark against depression. I groped, stumbled through my classes, through meetings, even continued to lecture at colleges. As the new year approached, however, and the school vacation enabled me to be completely alone, I wrote, sometimes, ten, twelve, fifteen hours a day. My mind boggled from the sheer weight of words. They were my soporifics, my opiate. They exhausted me and forbade me to dream. But which was worst? The work or the despair? This was the kind of despair I no longer enjoyed. There were no delirious, sweet moments as before. There was no longer elation to revel in, only despair to escape from. So I became a man chained to a typewriter. All movements and thoughts were conditioned by the typewriter. There was, however, no friendship between us; there was warfare and I knew that the typewriter would win, would survive me. On the other hand, the typewriter was my only friend. It was proof that I still functioned as a man, that I was. I reread, almost daily, the fruits of other typewriters, the books already written, and gained sustenance, renewed courage. The women, they came and went, but they were tarnished mirrors, reflecting images

I could no longer believe in. I would leave them and come back to my typewriter.

The days were not long enough. Night came, and with it, the darkness of the past. I was a constant dreamer of nightmares. In a frequent one, I am being buried alive; I feel myself enclosed in a narrow box; I do not cry for help because I do not want to be helped. I want to lie, frightened, terrified. In another, I am being chased by a blond Swede; his white hair resembles that of the Medusa; it is composed of many snakes. He has an accomplice, a Black woman. Together they subdue me, tie me up in chains; the snakes become whips, lashing my body. In still another nightmare, I am a preacher at my own funeral. I stand looking down upon my casket. I say, "I don't care what they say about him; he was not such a bad fellow. You know what Joe Pittman says, The poor boy did the best he could; well, you can't fault him, after all, that's all he could do, the best he could . . ."

Morbidity, depression, work. They were my trinity. They enabled me to move from day to night. They accounted, together, for my highs, coming infrequently now, and my lows, those times when I dashed from the typewriter, tears streaming down my face, the scream in my chest, to throw myself upon the bed, to choke on the tears of yesterday. My lows came more often, more damning, and they brought the anxiety and the dizziness, the severe pains in my abdomen; a simple thud from the apartment above drove hundreds of nails through my body. I awoke at night, struggling to reach the light after a nightmare, to plunge the darkness into light. The sounds of the typewriter, muffled, were like pinpricks on the edge of my brain. The unsteadiness came to my arms, my legs. I was like an old man. I was like one of the breathing dead. The physical pain was as severe as the mental pain. Still, I dreamed of dying, and dreamed of chaos and peace; and still journeyed down by the East River to stand beneath her window. I reread the old books over and over again; and I warred with the shadows, night and day—shadows without substance, and always it was they, atop me, holding me down, pummeling me . . . yes!"

CHAPTER 7

My days and nights changed little during the next four months, in which I moved always close to mental catastrophe, buttressed by alcohol and tranquilizers. My journal of the period—I managed to keep one, though I wrote only occasionally—is filled with notations on my lack of appetite, my long periods of sleeping, waking, and sleeping again, the decrease of my work output from twelve hours to half an hour daily, from twenty pages to one, and is capped by the admission of June 21, 1973: "Life in a flux, I am, I know, a sick man. I must unravel my life . . . I must become well."

At the age of forty, believing myself to have reached the feverish pitch of crisis, I went into therapy. The therapist, Raphael Rosell, was from South America. He had hypnotic eyes, a perpetual smile playing about the corners of his mouth, and hair cut short atop his head. I had long maintained a reservation about psychoanalysis, believing that only the weak sought such assistance, that I could deal with emotional problems by retreating into isolation. Raphael was an unorthodox therapist; the relationship he attempted to establish between himself and his patients was not that of father and son/daughter, but that of one friend to another. After two months, we had established a relationship moving along those lines, and I had become much calmer than I had been over the last year. Thus, having established a working relationship, the bulk of our work began in the fall of 1972.

At the beginning of September, three weeks before I was to

begin work at school again, the topic between us was feelings. I remember sitting in the easy chair, watching him unwrap, moisten, and then light a panatella. Finally, he turned to me, eyes flashing hypnotically: "Well, my friend, how are you?"

I responded automatically as usual, "Fine."

"Any thought about what we talked about last time?" I reached for my pipe, lit up, drew heavily. Last time and the time before, the subject had been the same—feelings. I had written the session up in my journal, and then forgotten about it. "I didn't come to any conclusions," I replied.

"Well, what do you think, if anything?"

"The same. I don't trust feelings. You can't live by them."

"Why are you so strongly against feelings, against being, as you call it, emotional?"

I relit my pipe. The answer was ready, yet the formulation and articulation of it was not for the therapist, but to be recorded in my journal. There I answered truthfully the questions I avoided during therapy. I had written of the last session: "It was feeling and emotion that sent me here to analysis in the first place. Having lost control, almost completely, for the second time in my life, I had come close to destroying myself." Fondling my pipe in my hand, I turned to Raphael, said, "Look, emotions, feelings, they are damn private things . . . things inside . . ."

He picked up the abrupt change in my voice. "Why are you so hostile?"

"Hostile?" I responded. I laughed nervously. "Why is it when I don't give you an answer you want, I'm hostile?"

He narrowed the distance between himself and me, bent closer. "Look, whenever we get on this subject, you'd like to tell me to go fuck myself, wouldn't you?"

I hesitated, thought, "Yes, I would." I stared at him without answering.

"Why don't you?" he persisted.

"Why should I?" I queried uncomfortably.

"You should if you want to. Why are you afraid to be angry, to let go, why so tight?"

I retreated by taking a long time to light my pipe. My mind went back to Walter, to the figure standing over top of him, me, to the animal I had become, and there was momentary panic at the thought of being angry with Raphael, of leaping the narrow space between us, of seizing him by the throat. I shuddered at the thought.

Placing his hands on my shoulder, looking directly into my face, he said softly, "We always come back to it sooner or later. There's all this feeling down there and, I think, a hell of a lot of anger too. You fight it, control it. Look, you've got marvelous control. But maybe you don't have to use all that energy controlling it. If we can find out what it is, why it's there . . ."

"All right!" I cut him short. "I know what you're saying; but I don't want to come—as you call it—in touch with my feelings."

"Why not?"

"Because I did about four months ago, and I ended up here."

"Addison," he interjected briefly, "cut the bullshit. Maybe you had a nervous breakdown, were about to have one. I thought so at first. Maybe you thought you could make things up to your wife by having a nervous breakdown. Now, I'm not sure whether you would or not—I mean have had a breakdown."

The answer rolled defiantly from my lips: "You're damned right, I wasn't going to have a breakdown!"

I was surprised that he seemed to believe me; I did not think I believed myself.

"Why?"

"Because . . . because . . . Look, I just wasn't!"

"You mean you were going to control your feelings come hell or high water?"

The panic showed through my response. "Look, will you get off this stuff about feelings? I've told you, in this white people's country, Black people don't walk around with their feelings on their shoulders. You'd better be thinking most of the time."

Agitated, he threw up his hands. "The white people again. I talk to you about *your* feelings and you start talking about white people."

Laughingly, I remembered that he once called me the artful dodger. I had made him uncomfortable now. Not being a native American he knew about the racial situation only second-hand. In this area, I was the expert. "Because," I replied, "if you want to talk to me about feelings or anything else, you have to come to racism in this country. I know that damn much. Let your feelings go, laugh, be happy around white people and they try to take advantage of you; exhibit your anger, let out the rage, get in touch with your feelings, as you call it, and you end up killing one of them. No, if you're a Black man in this country and you want to survive, you keep it inside."

His voice became soft, slightly sarcastic. "But, Addison, you are scared to death of Black men too. But look, I'm not talking about the political situation, not about Black men or white men, but about you—why all the control, why so tight?"

There was a kindness, almost a pleading tone in his voice, in his eyes. The seriousness was there too. I looked away from him, out at the East River. A boat passed by. White clouds and blue sky appeared in the distance. Suddenly I felt very tired, moved my eyes back to his face, said, more softly now, "Because I didn't want to have a nervous breakdown."

"Why not?" he asked softly, tenderly.

"I didn't want to lose my mind," I said.

"What do you think will happen if you lose your mind?"

"I don't know."

"Have you ever seen anyone, known anyone to lose his mind?"

"I don't know."

"What do you think happens when people lose their minds?"

"They become like children."

"What's wrong with being a child?"

The boat had disappeared. The river was calm, peaceful. "Children are helpless; they can't protect themselves and nobody else will do it for them. In this world, you'd better be able to protect yourself."

That night, I wrote in my journal: "Raphael is not a bad person, but I should stop going to see him. Yes, he was right, I am afraid of Black men too. So what? He knows it and I know it. Why doesn't he explain it? Why do I have to do all the work? He makes me damn uncomfortable; first about being in competition with my father, now about feelings. I don't know what he means —get in touch with your feelings. What the hell do I do? Do I push a switch, turn a button? And what does it matter if I keep my feelings to myself? Why should I make a public disclosure of them? Why should I use them the way women do—to blackmail people, to cause guilt, gain pity? And he knows that I am not a machine, that I have feelings. Yes, I *do* feel pain, love, remorse. I do!"

One of the most crucial sessions, as I saw it, occurred later, near

the end of the month, after I had settled back into the routine of
teaching. Back again in the soft easy chair, I looked away from
Raphael, out again toward the East River. The sky was dark, a
trickle of rain fell on the tall buildings some few yards from the
window. Raphael puffed on his cigar; I lit my pipe.

"Well." He waved the cigar in my direction—the cue for me to
begin talking.

I rested the pipe on the metal ashtray. "I had . . . a funny kind
of experience—in class today."

"Do you want to talk about it?"

I did. I looked past his eyes, flashing alive now, to a blank spot
on the wall near the window. I was back in the classroom. I was
teaching the novel *Native Son*. I moved from the desk to the
blackboard, wrote the words "gratuitous murder" on the blackboard. I explained the meaning of the term to the class. "For
years Bigger lived with pent-up rage inside of him, hatred, a wish
to murder. Remember our discussion of *Germinal*, and the coal
miner Bonnemort. The situation is analogous: all of their lives
these men were brutalized by society, all of their lives, they longed
for revenge. The longing is part of their blood, flows in their
veins, as the energy that drives them from day to day. Murder is
the organizing principle of their lives, their subconscious lives, and
if they live long enough and circumstances arise, one day they will
give way to their passions, commit murder—out of rage and
hatred." I had moved to the far side of the room, near the window. I was about to begin further explication of Bigger's crime
when, suddenly, I felt faint, dizzy, my legs began to wobble, my
heart pounded faster, faster, and, talking rapidly, I moved to my
desk, flung a question out to the class, with trembling hands lit
my pipe.

"How long did this feeling last?" asked Raphael.

"Not long. Maybe a minute, maybe less."

"Has it happened before, in class?"

"Yes, a long time ago."

"Did the students know?"

"No, I covered it very well."

"What do you think triggered it off?"

"I don't know."

"Could it have been the story?"

"I don't know why. I've taught this novel, God knows how many times."

"Did something happen before class? Yesterday, even that morning?"

He paused, relit the panatella. I took advantage of the break to relight my pipe. The rain fell more heavily, water bounced from the roofs of tall buildings; the East River seemed to have disappeared under a cloak of darkness. I remembered that I had once thought of drowning in that river.

"We've been talking all along about feelings," Raphael began again, "emotions, rage, and anger. Is that what the novel is about?"

"Yes."

"Could there be some connection there?"

Thoughtfully, I puffed on the half-lit pipe. There was, I supposed, a connection, but I didn't know how to explain it. "At the end of the novel," I said, "Bigger Thomas goes to the electric chair. I think that I might have thought about that."

"I don't understand."

"Well . . . if you were Black in the South and you committed a crime against white people, you went to the electric chair. That's how it was. Almost everybody in our neighborhood had heard of someone who had gone to the electric chair. So if you were a bad boy, the old people would say that you were going to the electric chair."

"And you were told this?"

I remembered the madonna, her shrieks, her screams, the dreaded words. "Yes, a lot of times, by a lot of people."

"Why, what did you do?"

"Nothing really. I was kind of hardheaded, smart, thought I was different."

"So what?"

"So, sooner or later, they thought I would end up in the electric chair. My family, teachers, older people in the neighborhood. They were trying to protect me, I guess."

"From what?"

"From white people. I guess they thought that if I continued being different, sooner or later, I would get into trouble."

"You hated them then? Now you're protecting them?"

"I never hated them all."

"No, but a lot of them, you thought they were your enemies."

"I understand them better, now."

"Or you're ready to forgive them?"

I lapsed into silence.

"Well, all right. But you said they wanted to protect you? Couldn't it have been that they didn't want you to be different?"

"It might have been."

"And so if you were different, you would be punished?" He paused, looked down at the space near my feet, brought his eyes slowly to mine. "And being different means to be an individual, saying what you want to, doing what you want to, acting for yourself? Right?" He did not wait for my reply, his eyes narrowed, became slits, hard. "In other words, to be different meant to be white. White people were smart, white people could talk back, say what they wanted, do what they wanted, be different. If Black people like you—not mulattoes, though that's another thing—we call them *assimillados*—do this, they are acting like white people. Is it possible you were being punished, being mistreated, harassed, for acting like white people?"

The pipe rested in the metal ashtray. I thought about his summation, rolled the words around in my mind. Is that what my father had recognized, years ago, when he had asked me why I wanted to be white? But also, did being an individual mean being white? Did not wanting to be ugly, not wanting to be Black, wanting to be mullato, did this equal wanting to be white? "Maybe," I answered Raphael and myself, affirmatively, "maybe I was acting like white people."

"And you still are, aren't you?"

I was surprised by the question. I had thought, since Seattle, that I had moved outside of the patterns of old, had at least wanted to. "Do I?" I asked, unsure.

"Well . . . think about it. You're a professor in a white university. You're a writer, internationally known. You wear expensive clothes, live in a white neighborhood. You lecture at well-known white colleges, sit on committees, people come to you for advice, help, who knows?—all of these are things that white people do, aren't they?"

The answer of course was yes. I thought of a co-worker, who wanted to be a full professor, and I was amused; I had never expected to be a professor at all—assistant or associate, let alone a full professor. Such jobs were those white people dreamed of. Nothing in my experience made me want to strive for such positions. I had become an associate professor by accident, not by design.

Alone with my journal the next night, I tried to put the pieces together. "My father had been right, after all. He had known, perhaps, much better than I, that the mulattoes were not the real targets, as I had believed. He had known. And had expected me to know that they had had no real power. They were surrogates, wielding power at the behest of others; their arrogance was a counterfeit arrogance, based not so much upon just deserts, but upon the benevolence of white people. They were not the rose, had only been close to the rose, and for me to go beyond them, to achieve victory over them, to defeat them meant to want to be what white people were, what they symbolized. It meant, finally, to want to be white. This meant moving outside of one set of patterns and trying to live within the rules of another. And there was no middle ground; each option meant betrayal, each had its own rules of punishment. Very well. I no longer have to accept either option. I have more realistic images now. I know much more of Frederick Douglass and Martin Delany, of W. E. B. Du Bois and Henry Highland Garnet, of Harriet Tubman and Sojourner Truth. *And if I were a betrayer before, I am no longer, and I will no longer feel guilty; I am not a white man; I am a Black man.*"

If, as I had believed, the chances of mental disaster had been outstanding in the spring and summer of 1972, here, in the winter of the same year, they were minimal. I was still afflicted by short bouts of depression, but they were neither of long duration nor very severe. The very thought of suicide became abhorrent to me, and gradually I became less of a recluse, willing to move outside the isolation and alienation I had once coveted so much. I accepted my appointments to committees, both in the university and in the college itself as something more than formal positions, and worked enthusiastically at committee assignments. I wrote more surely and steadily, and by October, I had finished work on the history of the Black novel. I accepted positions on Black magazines as a contributing editor that I would not have accepted before, and I dated often with a passion almost completely lacking in the past.

Two days after Thanksgiving, however, an incident occurred which sent me once again into severe despair and made me seek a session with Raphael outside our normal schedule. David Lorrens had committed suicide. The official statement would always announce his death as an accident, would explain that his car had veered uncontrollably, forcing him into the crash which ended his life. Not long after I had left Seattle, David had suffered an emotional breakdown, had been forced into intense psychiatric treatment; for the past year his mental state had been kept in check by tranquilizing drugs.

I received the news of his death with stunning uncertainty. What did it all mean? How had it happened? Could it not also happen to me? Later that night, in an attempt to bolster my courage, I had written lines of bravado: "Every man must find his own nirvana; and no man can guide him there." The words could not mask the guilt I felt, however, the belief even that long ago, in the shadow of the white mountain, I might have said something, done something, to prevent this catastrophe. I remained away from school the next day, broke a date for the following night, walked again down by the East River. I thought of my father and of my former classmates in Virginia, now the breathing dead, and I realized anew how vulnerable we all were, how prone to overwhelming disaster. There were, I knew, no guarantees in life, no one was absolutely secure from calamity, but I knew also that for us, the strain and stress of living in this white country enhanced our odds twofold. Later, during the week, after having been unable to down the despair on my own, I called Raphael, made an appointment, told him about David, about my observations.

"Isn't it possible," he asked, after lighting the panatella, "that your depression has to do with you as much as David?"

"If you mean," I admitted, ashamed, "that I thought it might happen to me, too, sure."

"No," I don't mean that. "That's normal; but something else."

I could think of nothing.

He moved from the leather chair, retrieved an ashtray, came back to stare directly at me. "All your life you wanted to be a big shot, now you're a big shot, and it bothers the hell out of you."

I do not like the term "big shot," it grates on my nerves, conjures up despicable images. "I came to talk about David," I said angrily.

"Like hell. Look, cut out the bullshit. You came to talk about you. Let's talk about you." He waved away my interruptions. "You've been scared shitless all your life. If you're so goddamn scared, how do you protect yourself? And never mind the bullshit about white people—you wanted to protect yourself from every goddamned body."

"Why the hell are you so fucking uptight?" I interjected, forcefully.

"Who says I'm uptight?"

"You act like it."

"So what? Don't I have a right to be uptight?"

"Look." I extended a forefinger.

"No! You look! If I'm uptight, what the hell does it mean to you? Except maybe you think it's your fault that I'm uptight?"

I sat bolt upright in the chair. Of course I thought it was my fault. I thought I had offended him, made him angry.

"Like all big shots," he went on, "you wanted to be feared, and liked. And so when I don't smile at you, talk rationally to you, have a bad day, curse, it means that I don't like you. But what the hell should any of this have to do with you? I have my own life, my own problems, frustrations, everything that you have."

I sighed, turned away from him. I did not need him now, at this point in therapy, to spell it out for me. He had his own problems: so did the madonna, Rosalie, Yvonne, Ruth, my father, David.

"Now you see"—his voice became soft, compassionate—"what we've been getting at. All those defenses you erected as a child are still there. The needs too. How does a poor boy, Black or white, protect himself? He becomes a big shot. No one can touch him then. But if his defenses and needs remain the same, he can never be secure even as a big shot. He is still frightened; he thinks that something can still happen to him. In your case, there's something else: you not only had to save yourself; you had to save everybody: Rosalie, your mother, your sisters, your race, oppressed people, all your girl friends, David, God knows who else."

"Look," I shouted, not sure of what I wanted to say. "Look. I think *you're* crazy. Some of that stuff—the big shot thing—there may be some truth in some of that. But that saving stuff . . . Look, I'm a writer; I don't like to see people unhappy, abused, persecuted; there's not much I can do, I do what I can."

He scowled, brought his face close to mine. "You're not being honest. That's the old rationale. You wanted to save people because you thought you were responsible for them. And because of that, people have tricked you all of your life. You call it blackmail. But it worked both ways. I won't try to trick you—you've been tricked enough. But why the hell do you think you're responsible for what happened to other people? To Rosalie, your mother, your father, to David? You knew them for only a small part of their lives. You're like those mothers who come in here filled with guilt about their children, as if the children weren't open to other influences, as if what happened to them wouldn't have happened anyway. No, Addison, my friend, what happened to the people you know may have been bad, but you're not responsible. You're not."

"To assume responsibility for others," I confided later in my journal, "means to relieve the individual of responsibility for his own life, to seek to foster dependence and thereby control. People become abstractions, are transformed into objects of manipulation, are robbed of their humanity. Did I ever really believe it was my fault that David committed suicide, that Rosalie suffered? Or did I need to convince myself that I believed this? And how could I have made things different for either of them, how could I have dictated to them what their needs were, should have been, told them how to resolve their own conflicts? Neither would have listened to me, nor I to them. Both acted out of the patterns of their lives, confronted the terrors of living in the ways they knew best. In the battle against conflict they were their own best allies, and nothing that I could have done would have altered the outcome of their private wars. No, I could not save them. Only they could save themselves.

"I could offer solace, sympathy, compassion, comfort. But I could not fight their wars, could not save them; no, no more than I could save the madonna. How could I make her pain more bearable—was it ever as unbearable as I had imagined? And if I were incapable of saving her, what right did I have to censure her, to think of her as my betrayer? Had she no life beyond what she had brought into being, no needs that were not secondary to mine, no right to exist but as an appendage to me?

"But what did all of this mean now for me? What good did it do to understand the past patterns of my life? What was I supposed to do? I could not, perhaps, radically alter them, even though I wanted to. The defenses I had erected during childhood had worked. I did not go to the electric chair. To be sure, fear propelled me through a great many experiences, but had it not been for that fear and anger, would I have come through, survived? So what if for most of my life I had shied away from close relations, feared rejection, sought instead isolation, alienation? Had I not done so, would I have been able to get through school, would I have acquired the discipline necessary to write? But further, if not for the terror of living, could I have continued to live?

"Raphael talks about happiness. But what does this mean? I am not as unhappy now as I was before, not in such a continual state of panic. What happened to me in that Brooklyn precinct house could very well, I know, happen again, but if it did, somebody would take notice; my friends would write about it, make an issue of it. And so what if I used my status and reputation to protect myself? Everyone needs protection and it is difficult to get from inside only. Even Raphael. He is proud of being a psychologist, defines himself, at times, in this way. And then there are the white people I am always meeting, who attempt to impress me with their credentials, informing me of the books they have written, the positions of importance they hold.

"And if this is the norm for white people, why not for Black people? Being a writer and professor does not make me better than other Blacks, but it offers a minimal kind of protection that I had never had before. Addison Gayle the writer and professor differs from Addison Gayle the porter and orderly because the former can wrap himself in a cloak of security that the latter would be denied. And why should I not wear this cloak, so long as I do not lose sight of the basic reality: whenever the racial Armageddon comes, the common denominator for the writer and the porter is the blackness of the skins of both."

Crises like that generated by David's death were almost nonexistent over the following months, and those that did occur, involving chance meetings with Rosalie, or disappointment over a romantic affair, no longer rekindled the old despair. I was helped along toward emotional recovery by the kind words being written about me by friends (even the unkind ones, by enemies, delighted me) and others engaged in the area of Black literature. Lecture invitations came steadily now, along with job offers from major colleges. My book *The Black Aesthetic* had been translated into Japanese and became, according to one critic, the manifesto of a new critical movement in American literature. My sessions with Raphael had become more philosophical than analytical, devoted more to how I would handle myself in the future than to what had happened to me in the past. "Whatever happened to you back there," he had said, "I can help you understand, but neither I nor you can undo. Besides . . . we both know, don't we, that much of the past was manipulated by you, perhaps because you had to, but nevertheless, it was."

Looking back into the past from this vantage point, it was not difficult to conclude with him that I had been either ingeniously my own best ally or my worst enemy. I, too, doubted seriously now, if much of what had happened to me, if much of what I had considered crisis, had happened at all, been crises at all. Certainly, I had remained functional through everything, had never been completely immobilized, had used anger, fear, anxiety toward constructive ends. No, the past could not be undone, and I am not sure that I would want to undo it, that I would not, if given the option, relive it all over again. But it could be understood, and the way for me to do this was to do what I liked doing best—to write—this time to write about the past.

In 1971, after I had signed the three-book contract with Doubleday, the editor, Loretta Barrett, and I had decided that a series of personal articles, similar to those that I had compiled for *The Black Situation,* would constitute one of the books. Those articles had dwelt upon aspects of my past, had been autobiographical, but most of the essays had dealt with other topics, with literature, with the social and political aspects of the Black situation. In March of 1973, with the first book in the series, *The Way of the New World,* now behind me, and buttressed by the new more positive image of myself, I decided to write not a series of articles, but an autobiography in narrative form. During our March session, I effusively related my plans to Raphael.

"Maybe I'll begin with Seattle, with David and Rainier—I still see the mountain as a kind of rite of passage, see David as very important in everything. Then I'll use flashbacks, move backward to reveal as much of the truth as possible, try to place things in a rational, chronological order, move up through my life as an adult, come up to now, to the present."

"Are you a little scared?"

"I'm a lot scared. Not so much of confronting myself, but of confronting other people."

"How will you deal with that?"

"I don't know! I suppose I'll use images and symbols; words that say one thing and mean another."

"But you don't like that, do you?"

"No, it's dishonest. Writers, at least, should be honest."

Cynically: "Tell the truth, no matter what?"

"Well . . ." I thought of Leslie Berger. "Sometimes," he had said, "you hurt people by being honest." "As honest," I said, "as I can be."

"Do you see any dangers or rather, problems?"

"Only that much of it will be sad, I guess, to people who thought they knew me; but I don't think, on the whole, it will be sad."

"But your life has been, well, if not sad, certainly not very happy. The first book, as I remember, *The Black Situation*, that was sort of sad."

I recalled his comments after I discovered that he had gone to the library at the beginning of our sessions and read the book without my knowledge: "It was very touching." And I remembered the exhange that had followed:

Me: "I think it's funny."

Raphael: "Funny! I don't see a damn thing funny about your life!"

"If my life had ended," I continued explaining about the autobiography, "two years ago, last year, maybe my life would have been totally unhappy. I don't think so, but maybe you could say that it would have been. But nothing that has happened to me has not helped me. Everything, as I see it, has brought me to this point. Look: I've already lectured at four colleges this year. Three weeks from now, I go to a week-long seminar in Atlanta; two weeks after that I lecture again at the Sorbonne. If I hadn't had the kind of experiences I've had, hadn't undergone what I did, I might not be doing those things."

"On the other hand, you might not have had to . . ."

I repeated the words so often spoken between us, "Prove myself?"

"Yes."

"Maybe not. But maybe if I didn't have to prove myself, I wouldn't have lived. And I've lived. If I died today, I would know that I've lived. And, you know, I'm so sure that I want to be cured of what's bothering me. I don't want to be so afraid and I'm not so much anymore. I'm not so uptight anymore. But being Black in this country means to always be prepared for war; I don't ever want to lose that attitude."

"You're ready to leave therapy now, aren't you?"

I lowered my head guiltily. "I suppose so."

"Why don't you?"

"I don't know."

"You're not so dependent on me. You never were, on anybody. I think that you could do very well without me. If not, you can always come back."

"I don't have to make up my mind now, do I?"

"Of course not, my friend. Whenever you're ready."

We remained silent. I avoided his eyes.

"Do you agree me with me now," he changed the subject, "that you're different from other people not because you're Black, but because you're a writer?"

"Well . . ." I began hesitantly, relieved that we were moving to already covered ground.

"Don't think of being different as being weird or better than someone else. That's part of your hangup. Things are either one way or another. Think of different as having a sensitivity, an insight that maybe other people don't have. Maybe artists are different from other people, maybe you are different because you do something with your hangups, make them work for you."

This subject had constituted one of our most heated sessions. Afterward, I had written in my journal: "Why does Raphael want to make me less Black? I am not different from other Black people, only luckier. The feeling, the sensitivity is there, in each of us, but it comes out in different ways. Had I remained at the Brooklyn Army Base, never moved outside, I might have gone to jail or, worse, the electric chair. The anger and rage that goes into writing might have pushed me into other directions, might have made me a real Bigger Thomas. In becoming a writer, I simply rebelled in a much more socially acceptable way. This constitutes a difference, if at all, in terms of degree: the man who can murder on the printed page can do so time and time again and need not fear jail or death.

"But writing is not all about anger and rage, death and murder. It is also about love and compassion, about living and hoping. It is about morality and justice, about positive relationships between one human being and another, about beauty and splendor, about success and victory, about empathy and feeling; it is an attempt to make sense out of the absurdity of one's experiences. It is, to quote Baldwin, an act of love. And in this sense, maybe Raphael, with Freud, is right; perhaps those who see, simultaneously, both beauty and ugliness, hatred and love, who feel anger and rage at the injustices leveled against people by others, who wish to interject a new sense of morality into the world, maybe such people are different. Maybe I am, in a sense, different from other people."

Still, sitting there looking at Raphael, it was difficult for me to voice aloud what I had written in my journal. I banged my pipe out in the metal ashtray, nodded in agreement, said by the shake of my head that I conceded my difference.

"Do you," he moved on, "think that you can deal with Rosalie now, truthfully, I mean, with your marriage, in a book?"

I avoided giving him a direct answer. We debated the question for the remainder of the session, but he knew as well as I that the real answer was not for his ears, but for the blank pages of my journal. That night, a bottle of wine at my elbow, I wrote: "The real problem is not so much Rosalie, but the guilt. The breakdown or near breakdown occurred because of the picture I had in my mind of myself. I thought of myself as a criminal, as one who had committed a crime. Yet, even if this were so, did the punishment fit the crime? Should I have been reduced almost to insanity for terminating a relationship? Suffering, I suppose, was natural, but at some point the suffering need end, the world had to be put back together again, life had to continue.

"And so it had to be for both of us. But I prolonged the suffering in my own mind. I conjured up fantasies of her in which she underwent the most terrible experiences—psychological, even physical injury—and all the time I was certain that none of this could happen to me, that I could not really be forced across the threshold of insanity. I could not allow such strength for her, could only view her as a pitiable child, destroyed by my criminality. I imbued her with my own feelings, molded her, made her a surrogate of my imagination. But she is a woman of tremendous strength. She has lived, survived, and her world has not come to an end. She set about with determination to put her world back together again, while I have only begun to do the same. And yet both of us stepped outside of our histories, breaking with traditions that had mentally enslaved us. We both came to realize that life was, above all, chaos and tumult—whatever order could be imposed, would be imposed by the individual. Two lovers, even, could determine the destinies not of each other, but of each singly, and this could be done only by facing the horrendous ordeal of the past.

"Four months ago I could not call your name without feelings of self-pity, self-hatred, guilt and despair. Today, however, I can write about you, picture you not as abstraction, but as a human being; and instead of a sense of guilt, now, I feel a sense of loss for what might have been. But I know what there was, sometimes, despite all else. I recall still the gaiety and laughter, the dreams and the hopes; and then I am alive with the sense of living, of self-worth, of good feeling; and it is then that I realize that I have crossed the Rubicon."

CHAPTER 8

In April I traveled to Atlanta, Georgia, to participate in the annual Black writers' conference, held at Clark College, under the
auspices of the English department. The morning after I arrived,
I sat in the restaurant of the hotel in which I was registered, eating breakfast with novelist Sam Greenlee, another participant. I
remembered that this was my first trip South in two years, that I
had not been home for that length of time despite entreaties from
my mother. This was my second visit to Atlanta. On the first,
some three years before, I had participated in a conference at
Morehouse College, had remained only a few hours. This time I
was to remain for an entire week, and I confided to Sam that I
had not spent an entire week in the South since leaving over
twenty-five years ago.

I was like the prodigal come home, filled with a sense of wonder and surprise. I marveled at the southern drawl of the people
surrounding us in the restaurant, of the openly flirtatious mannerisms of the beautiful women, the quick masculine strides of the
men, the hustle and bustle, the good-natured friendly greetings,
open back-slapping, unself-conscious laughter; these for me were
remembrances of things past.

Julian Bond came to our table, introduced himself, sat down.
"Visiting my constituency," the young legislator said. His presence at our table attracted other politicians and soon there was a

discussion about civil rights, Atlanta, political power. The discussion was open, frank. The men, assured, confident.

"How much," the poet Claude McKay, recalling Jamaica, the place of his birth, had once asked in one of his most celebrated poems, "have I forgotten?" Sitting there now, watching Black men, resplendent in three-button suits, flirting courteously, openly, with the pretty waitresses, I recalled those words, and asked them silently of myself.

How much have I forgotten of genuine emotions, of honest feelings, of candor and sincerity? How much have I forgotten of a people who themselves never forgot how to dream? With some sense of shame, I recalled that in essay after essay I had written cynically of the southern Martin Luther King, the epitome of the dream. In so doing, I had forgotten that the dream was an integral part of our heritage, that we are a people who, during the worst of times, had never stopped believing in the dream, that such beliefs had been handed down to us from our warriors of old —from David Walker and Henry Highland Garnet, from Bishop Richard Allen and Samuel Cornish, from Sojourner Truth and Harriet Tubman, from Martin Delany and Frederick Douglass— and that the dream had been and remained our chief line of defense, the bulwark against the horrible exigencies of the American experience, the propelling force, ushering us through the catacombs of American history.

Here was the great strength of a people, and here was, perhaps, my great weakness. I had allowed the dream to degenerate into cynicism, had begun to laugh at both the dream and the dreamers, and in doing so, had negated a large part of my own heritage. Having lost cognizance of the dream, I had forgotten much of my own history. At the table now, there were three mulattoes, Bond included, and four Blacks. Outside of myself, no one, I suppose, acknowledged or thought of the color composition of the group. These were men, secure in themselves, filled with a sense of purpose, and they regarded each other not as mulattoes or browns, but as Blacks. And somewhere, I recalled even in my past, in Newport News, Virginia, despite the artificial barriers created by a few, there were those whom I never defined in the American way—according to the texture and color of their skin— those like Patricia, and Red Drag, and Tillie, and the numerous friends of my mother and my father, who treated me well, who were concerned about my welfare.

How much forgotten? I had forgotten that beyond all, there existed between us, between those with dark skins and those with light ones, an idea of brotherhood, immune to artificial barriers; that sometimes men and women did what they had to, but in so doing, most never lost sight of the common purpose. I had forgotten also that alongside the trauma of adolescence, the many days of despair and anguish, the feelings of rejection and self-doubt, there were other feelings and other days, sunshine days, when:

I lay on my back, exhausted after football practice, looking up into the sky, feeling tired and good and relaxed: I would sit in the back seat of the car—as my mother and father sat in the front— and watch the evergreen trees rapidly disappearing before my eyes and I would laugh with astonishment . . . My mother would make ice cream and I would turn the handle for hours at a time, it seemed, and be given, as reward, the spoon to lick.

The neighborhood was filled with the joyful-mournful sound of the Dixie Hummingbirds blaring from the radio of almost every house on the neighborhood.

I would sit in the garden with a girl, reciting poetry from memory, sometimes forgetting the lines, causing both of us to burst into laughter.

I would take my sisters on the ferry running between Newport News and Norfolk and be warmed by their enthusiasm and energy.

I would be commended by a teacher for having written a good essay or a good test paper.

I would play some prank on a classmate or a friend.

I would be rewarded for winning a spelling contest or doing well in the high school drama production.

I would be fed beer and wine by the pimps and prostitutes.

I would walk through the neighborhood at six o'clock in the morning singing at the top of my voice.

I would win money at craps and split my winnings with my friends.

I would mix mud with the snow and after wounding an opponent in our daily wars, call it quits and retreat to the safety of my house.

I would bank the wood stove in the front room at night and sit beside the big-bellied stove, reading a book, or writing a poem. Days when . . . And despite the conversation continuing around me, I recalled them now, remembered so much forgotten. The setting here in Atlanta undoubtedly had something to do with this: the dust-caked roads, the split in the concrete where the pavement ended, the small houses where humanity was, where sorrow was, but also where so much joy was, the town with one main street where people congregated, came together, laughed, fought, drank, the small churches where Black people lent their voices to the night—these were remnants of my/all our southern past. But most important, there were the people: the students and teachers, workers and politicians, poor people and more affluent ones, their lives tied together by a similar history and a similar destiny and who, despite or maybe because of the brutality practiced one against another, the many betrayals, despite all of this and more, remained such as dreams were built upon.

They were our/my forgotten past. Many of my colleagues, Black writers of the sixties and seventies, are Southerners. Like me, however, they have written little of these people, whom we knew, loved, and hated, believing, perhaps, that in their lives drama, excitement, and struggle were minimal. Our literature has followed the great migration of the twenties, choosing the urban center, as its locale, electing Bigger Thomas as an accurate paradigm of the Black condition. The true hero was the anti-hero, the Black of the city streets, who was buffeted and subdued by a hostile environment, pushed by psychological and sociological factors beyond his control into anti-human, anti-social acts.

Rebellion, as defined by the Americans, became an objective correlative of Black life in the sixties and early seventies. We were, they said, angry people (this was and remains true) programmed to wreak havoc upon white society; we were urban gorillas to some, fanatical white-haters to others, natural-born criminals to many, and to still others, degenerates, immoral men and women, attuned, as Norman Mailer implies in *The White Negro* to the "worst of perversion, promiscuity, pimpery, drug addiction, rape, razor slash, bottle-break, what have you. . . ." Here in the South, however, Black people adhered to their own definitions, set about creating a revolution not spectacularly in most instances, but determinedly and purposefully. They continued to preach the verities of old, would not accept the drug pusher, hustler, or fanatic as anything less than a distortion of the human personality, refused to grant such people the status of romantic rebels.

Having been workers for all of their lives, they believed in the work ethic, primarily because they refused to accept the largesse of their oppressors. To be sure they had not rid the South of drug addicts, criminals, hustlers; they knew, however, what the sociologists and urbanologists pretended not to know: that such constituted a very small minority among them; that most Black people lived desperate poverty-stricken lives and yet continued to work at meager occupations—washing and scrubbing the floors of white people, cooking their meals, running their industrial machines, never, along the way, committing acts of aggression or criminality; they continued in their quiet way to maintain dignity and a sense of purpose, dreaming always of the day when their sons and daughters would be able to leave the white people's kitchen forever.

I was jolted back to the present by a newcomer, who approached our table. He was a young man, around my age, similar to me in height and build, a politician, running in this year's congressional election. He wore his well-tailored suit with an air of self-confidence. His speech was soft, southern, imbued with the imagery and rhythm of Black speech from one southern locale to another. His gestures exuded composure and certainty. Quietly, I reflected that he was a man to whom the analyst's couch would be anathema. He would have little need for the Raphaels of this world, not because he would never confront turmoil and inner conflict, but because he had not forgotten a heritage which taught him to control and contain hurt and pain, to forge from them, instruments to fit his own needs. Like those of the town in which I was born, he knew that conflict and turmoil were necessary appendages, that each Black child must learn early the means of confronting them and subduing them. We are, Imamu Baraka has written, a blues people. Looking at the young politician, I was convinced of that fact. He appeared to me much like a blues poem, reminding me that the blues is a distinctive southern Black creation. Its practitioners were the poor man's Freud and Jung, who led a people to voice their frustrations, to view them openly and unashamedly, to weep, laugh, voice the hurt within, allowing people to undergo a catharsis more quickly than that sought after by the northern analyst. Unlike myself, the young politician had not forgotten the heroic stock from which he came, had not become urbanized to the extent that he placed more faith in modern technology than he did in himself. Self-reliance remained the code word by which he and others reorganized their lives, and faith and belief in one's own integrity and possibilities, the vehicles propelling them throughout the American experience. They had not forgotten how to cry; but more important, they had not forgotten how to laugh.

Abruptly, the laughter ended! All eyes turned, quickly, to the young woman who approached, touched my elbow, stood to my right. The group of men, almost as one, eyes flashing flirtatiously, arouse to offer their seats. I was the architect of their disappointment! I said good-by to Sam, leaving for a vacation in the Caribbean, introduced Brenda around, and escorted her from the restaurant. It was almost time for the morning seminar to begin, for me to offer my paper on "The Black Artist and the Creative Experience."

We were two Black rafts amidst a sea of blackness. Beautiful in figure and form, her skin the rich black of southern legend and folklore, her slim figure was draped in a dress of African print; her hair was braided into intricate designs. From the hotel to the campus, I was impressed by endless rows of dark faces, the prismlike sea of colors, dark brown, light brown, black, yellow, each part of a kaleidoscope, a tributary stream leading to one major river. I recalled, sarcastically, and mentioned the fact to Brenda, that after some fifty lectures, this was my first extended tour at a Black college in a setting exclusively Black, one in which whites did not intrude. My bitterness was apparent. How much would such sessions, such gatherings, have meant to me in the past? This energy, this vitality, emanating from the students might long ago have affected me, forced me to think about my estrangement from my own history. I am, however, seldom invited to lecture at Black colleges, despite my desire to be so invited, and for this, I have lost far more than the students.

For it means something to appear before a gathering of Black people, to be with them in a setting where there are no whites, where they honestly and sincerely debate the issues, answer the tough questions, issue the challenging statements. Too long isolated in this white world, it inspires something in me that goes beyond a simple return to roots. It means to be in touch with a special kind of energy, radiating from the prayer which begins every gathering to the singing that accompanies it. It means to be regarded by the young not with awe and condescension, but as one Black person who, despite what others might call "my accomplishments," despite even what I might take them to be, who, whether I want to acknowledge it or not, belongs to them and vice versa. For there is an umbilical cord uniting us which has been forged out of a common history, and whether I know it or not, like it or not, the cord can never be cut.

The message in their young voices, their eyes, came through loud and clear: you belong to us; we can fight you, challenge, defy you, correct you. But polished English, Brooks Brothers suit, New York address, and all, you are a part of this southern dust, of its energy and vibrancy, part of our songs and rhythms, despairs and joys. Somewhere, sometime, eons of years ago, our ancestors strode jointly from the white men's ships in chains. After many years, we proceeded to begin the creation of a new world, not singularly, but in unison, and so despite the difference between us in experiences, in age or sophistication, in accomplishment or in ideology—despite all this—like those, our first ancestors, we are bound, inseparably, one to the other.

Feet moving, perhaps too rapidly! Arms swinging wildly above my head. This, I said to my student partner, is the Addison Gayle version of the funky chicken. Our laughter was smothered by the rich harmonious chords of the Chanteles, a local singing group, composed of two men and two women—one, a male, a member of the college music department. The intellectual part of the program was over. The students had heard some of the best of the Black writers; they had listened to Sam Greenlee, Toni Cade, and John Killens, among others. Now the program was capped with music and dance—a party for the writers and students alike. Their warmth, their gaiety, their enthusiasm was infectious.

And I, with places to go and things to do, grasped this moment of respite. What did it matter that I had never learned to dance, that I was always out of step with the music? What did it matter that I felt awkward, tense, as if all eyes were riveted upon me and my partner. It did not; no, neither to them, nor to me. They were not hung up on form and style, but instead, intent upon enjoying themselves, on freeing the body from inhibition, allowing it full sway, letting it move wherever it would. There would be time enough to deal with the niceties of form and style. At that time, especially for me, it was enough to be there, swinging the buxom student about, humming the notes of the music in my head, laughing, frolicking, flirting; it was enough to be able to be accepted among them, on their terms, to belong.

Back in New York, in isolation in my apartment, overlooking the steel and concrete, I wrote in my dairy: "With all my hang-ups, Black people in Atlanta made me feel as if I belonged, as if we belonged, to each other. Yes, I belong to them despite the fact that I have imbibed too much of the American's manners, education, and culture; still, despite this, I belong to them and they belong to me, and together, we belong to each other. And Raphael, this is, for me, the great catharsis: to know that there are people to whom I belong, that I am not regarded by them as either freak or wonder, but instead, regarded as their brother, that no matter the coming years of continual warfare with this country, whether win or lose, we belong to each other; yes, Blacks and yellows, old and young, descendants of a people who never lost faith in the human spirit, who never lost cognizance of the fact that people were capable of overcoming difficulties. They believed and we all believe still, in man's ability to transcend himself, and we are, if only in the beginning stages, people who, as the poet Haki Madhubuti put it, walk the way of the new world. Yes!"

The warm feelings brought on by my week's stay in Atlanta accompanied me across the ocean to Paris. My visits to the Sorbonne had become almost annual affairs, but I had never come to Paris so devoid of despair before, so intoxicated by the very fact of being alive. What had, before, been heartrending despair, especially the last summer, after the separation from Rosalie, was now something close to sweet melancholy. I was in love as I had never been before, with the streets, the age-old monuments, the cafes, the parks. The bright, clear days caused reflection, thoughtfulness, and even when those thoughts turned to Nana and Rosalie, they brought no pain.

I had first met Nana when we were both on the faculty of City College, after my marriage to Rosalie, after California. Tall and statuesque, with short, cropped hair and blue eyes, she was the epitome of the Danish advertisements featuring beautiful women. Ours had been a platonic affair—we were both married at that time—until 1972, when we had met on the Left Bank, just off Boulevard St. Michel. Her marriage had ended in total disaster, forcing her first back to her native Denmark, until she moved to Paris. We shared each other's grief, each other's despair, and despite our mutual past troubles, we managed to carve something beautiful and enduring out of that Paris spring. The problems which had beset me in my relationship with Pat, years before, did not plague me any longer, and I gave of myself with freedom, with abandon—as much as was possible under the clouds of anguish and despondency.

I had thought of joining her in exile, then, of becoming, as I had long ago been tempted to become, a man without a country, but I had surrendered the temptation, had given my lecture and returned to America. Standing in the center of a bridge off Place des Arts then, where we had stood often, blocks away from the noise and crowds of the sidewalk cafes on Boulevard St. Michel, I had scanned the Paris landscape, breathed in the fresh wholesome air. Off to my right, in the distance, stood the Eiffel Tower, etched dramatically against the sky. Moving far out, the endless waters of the Seine wound past multicolored, shingled buildings, and was stirred now and then by the churning from a *bateau-mouche*—the tourist boat—or an affluent pleasure cutter. On my left were the spirals of the Notre Dame Cathedral and, beyond, more multicolored, shingled buildings. Down below, on the parapets running beneath the many bridges, stood tattered fishermen, their bent poles searching desperately for the small, minnow-like fishes that helped, here, in this inflation-ridden city, to supplement their diet.

Yes, I had thought very seriously of exile *then*, and the reason was not due solely to the breakup of my marriage, or to my mental state. Beyond my personal despair, there was that occasioned by the disappointments of the seventies, following so close upon the successes of the sixties, the return on almost all levels, to the old feelings of hopelessness, cynicism, and apathy, which, until the era of Martin King and Malcolm X, Stokely Carmichael, and H. Rap Brown, had so immobilized a race of people. This had been as true in the area of Black culture as it had been in the political sphere. I had remembered then that we had begun the great quest in *Black World* and *Liberator Magazine* to undo the works of such, even, as my old idol Richard Wright, to create a literature which would truthfully explicate the lives and experiences of a people who had heroically survived the American nightmare. We had raised aloft the banner of collectivity, pledged ourselves to warfare, not against each other, but against the eternal antagonist. Then, in 1972, the dream had ended. Hope had proven an ephemeral thing.

Already actions were being set in motion which, only a year hence (in 1973) would force Black writers, old allies, those who had pledged to adhere to the old formula, who seemed to have agreed on a common course, into cruel internecine warfare. I had known then, and knew still, that Black people would survive the present schism, but it ceased long ago to be a question of survival. The question was survival on what terms? Americans would always need servants, alter egos, yardsticks of *imagined* incompetence by which to measure their own *real* incompetence. And we might, no we would, survive a thousand years in such roles.

But what ignominy? What insult to a people? To survive as servants, adopting the bad habits, the morals and vices of "the master." Was survival worth such a price?

I had had no answers then, have none now, though I was disheartened at the fulfillment of my prophecy, often brooded, silently and in sessions with Raphael, in intellectual gatherings with my friends, in essays and lectures, on the loss of that *élan vital* which had, seemingly, in the latter part of the sixties and the early part of the seventies, so propelled us.

I was not so quick to be overwhelmed now, or to dwell for long in despair, and thus when I showed up at the Sorbonne, at the classroom of Professor Michel Fabre, a critic and writer on Black literature, in the summer of 1973, I was in good spirits. I had, after all, flirted with the pretty girls in the cafes, drunk wine in the restaurants, lounged in the parks, made pilgrimages from the Eiffel Tower to Notre Dame, revisited the places I had once visited with Rosalie and Nana. I had gone to Place Pigalle and flirted with the prostitutes, moved on to the artists' colony at Montmartre, climbed the hill with a Black schoolteacher and deserted her for an African tourist, a beautiful woman from Nigeria—who listened to my conversation, drank my wine, and left me to rejoin her classmates. And I had laughed with the laughter of old.

Now, facing the students, fresh from my triumph at Atlanta, I was still laughing, inwardly, the laughter of one satisfied with himself. The boy once destined for the electric chair was again giving a lecture at the Sorbonne, on Black poetry. I was introduced as a well-known critic, an expert, and the students, like those at other colleges and universites, regarded me with that respect reserved for well-known critics and experts. I smiled, thought of Raphael: he would be pleased to see me this way—almost effusive, the high not feigned or manufactured, but springing from a good feeling inside.

Contemporary poetry by African-Americans was the subject of my lecture, and I had chosen to devote my lecture to the works of Askia Muhummed Toure, whose volume *Songhai* had moved and impressed me. Askia, like few others of my contemporaries, had retained the vision of yesteryear, the faith and hope engendered in the sixties and early seventies, before the merchants with their superflys and corregidoras and sweetbacks, their esoteric life-styles and their cynicism had sought to destroy a cultural movement. I tried to impart something of this faith and belief, of which I myself am doubtful, to French and African students, tried to tell them something of what *Songhai* means. The book had captured a great deal of the meaning of the Black aesthetic movement. The poetry of Askia was the poetry of love and faith, poetry so antithetical to the spirit of America; it was poetry which spoke of values and morals in terms so explicit that to understand the message, one need only realize that men were responsible for one another, that each man was, indeed, his brother's keeper.

Here was the moral postulate of this terror-ridden age, the one objective worthy of man's striving and bother, the true light at the end of the tunnel. It was hewn out of a faith built upon a belief in human possibilities—in the ability of people to transcend their own mundanity. Years of living among the Americans had convinced many of us that the Americans were too far gone, too degenerate, to accept such moral postulates, that theirs was and would remain the morality of their lily-white churches and codes which enabled them to assign the cause of human misery to others, the sufferers, as if these, in their suffering, had violated the moral injunction. They prided themselves, the Americans, upon their generosity, boasted loudly of their care packages and their food for peace programs, even as they rationalized the murder and exploitation of people throughout the world by their emissaries.

No, there were no lessons on morality and ethics to be learned from the Americans. But among Black people, among a people who, despite all, continued to hope and believe in the coming of a better world—who even in the face of police dogs, even while confronting the nightstick of county sheriffs, the demagoguery of politicians, the brutality of night riders, chanted still the songs and words of lovers and reached out to embrace all of humanity— here a foundation for a new morality might be laid. It was a mighty vision and Askia had not forsaken it. It remained still the finest exponent of a value system which might, yet, in the purifying Jihad, purify the universe.

The applause from the students was loud, sustained, but I did not know whether or not they were able to glimpse this vision, did not know but what my own ambivalence might have prevented them. I was not sure that, with the dark clouds all around, I had not fallen by the wayside, had not perhaps, arrived at the cynical conclusion that mankind is everywhere the same and that in a universe of men, individual salvation was the only possibility. I was not sure, now, that what I had witnessed at Atlanta was not mere illusion, that I had not as of old, imposed my needs, wants, and desires upon events and people and ignored the reality, hidden myself from it. Did I, therefore, I wondered, see in Atlanta only what I wanted to see, feel only what I needed to feel? Is there any longer hope for us on a collective level, or have we not, perhaps, been so long among the Americans that we have become like them? Is it that I no longer retain the old fascination for dreams and visions, am no longer so enamored of the possibility that new worlds might be carved from the debris of the old, no longer hopeful that the war against racism and injustice will be won by those who hold aloft the banner of love and faith and humanity?

Outside, I moved away from the university, my hosts, the students. The Eiffel Tower was in lights, the daytime spectators having surrendered the tower to the men and women of the night. Dressed in evening gowns and dinner jackets, they were ushered up in the lifts (which during the day creaked slowly under the weight of too many tourists) to the fashionable dining room overlooking the city. Noises came from everywhere—from the cafes on St. Michel and St. Germain, from the crowds along the narrow streets of the Algerian quarter. For the first time that evening, I noticed the emergent Paris moon, crystallizing the Seine, freezing it in splotches of dark blue and hazy white. I moved on. Past the gardens, the bookstalls, the hawkers, the students on the make, the old voyeurs, peeping into the darkened emptiness of the Rectory on St. Sevann; the blue-coated, mustachioed police, barking orders in angry French, edging the people on, sometimes pushing them into the streets, where the cars sped by at incredible speeds.

I thought of the pretty graduate student from Chad who had questioned me—too long and too intensely, it seemed—after the session, long after the others had departed. I had taken her telphone number, but had neglected to push my advantage further. I should, I thought, have asked her to come with me, to share my melancholia. But why? She is still in love with dreams. She believes in the eventual salvation of her people, like Askia, holds fast to the romantic vision. She is still young, but despite my success with therapy, I am an old man. Already the dreams are beginning to fade. They are vibrant today, dormant tomorrow. I think about Raphael, remember that it is, perhaps, ironic that things that yesterday might have driven me close to tears, now only left me a little saddened, a little weary. It was proof, I suppose, that I had truly achieved a new sense of myself, had ridden down the demons of fear and anxiety, but was it possible that in so doing, I had lost the desire to dream, to fantasize, to make the impossible, possible. Is it possible that I had become the cynic, I who had once been the romantic?

The Cathedral of Notre Dame stood before me, its lighted spires touched also by the hazy white rays of the Paris moon. My mind went back to Chartres, to the cathedral there. Notre Dame appeared neither so stately nor so old, and though also aged might be called, in comparison, modern. But it had survived the Revolution and the Germans, war, chaos, turmoil, and stood, still stately and strong, defying even the elements and the crowds who traverse its somber interior, as if determined to exist forever. Yes, the cathedral is timeless, ageless, and yet measured in terms of the history of the world, not much so. And measured alongside human history, even less so. But what did this mean to me and why was I thinking so much of time and age? There is a section in Askia's book: time is set many years in the future; man has undergone a great transcendence, has brought into being the new man, has completed the conquest of Songhai.

I moved on, my eyes lingering still on the lighted spirals, to the park in front of the cathedral, felt the breeze coming up from the Seine, heard the muffled hum of the *bateaux-mouches* over the sounds of gaiety coming from the tourists packed tightly upon their decks. Was this the reason for your continual faith, hope, Askia? Did you find it possible to cling to the old vision because you understood the secret of time, the meaning of the ages? Do you remember still what some of us, in our haste and desperation often tend to forget: that in terms of history, *my great-grand-father was a slave*—that we are only three generations removed from iron and chains? If we think back only one hundred years or so, we realize that our great-grandparents were the property of other men, and that despite this, despite the violence and the brutality visited upon their offspring ever since, transcendence has taken place. Have you come to realize that one lives and acts not so much for the present but for the future, that only in the personal realm does the admonition of Goethe hold: "If I can say to the fleeting hour, remain, so fair thou art remain"? . . . one measures the life-span of individuals in temporal terms, but races and monuments are measured in terms of eternity, and over a stretch of time, neither lose for long, their intrinsic dignity. And do you know and believe still that it is the job of the writer, the poet, to make manifest this dignity, to imprison in words for the coming generations, the records of human triumphs and victories as well as setbacks and defeats? Do you know that it is the writer's job to define in the human personality, the heroic and enduring, thus assuring faith in the possibilities of the future?

No, it is not that Songhai is incapable of achievement, but only that men have never, before now, tried so hard to achieve it. Before we can bring the new world into being, we must shed the garments of the old. And we are a people who have shed many garments in the past, and so why not hold to the belief that such is also possible in the future? Perhaps, then, all that I saw and felt at Atlanta was real, as real as the warfare between old allies, as real as the more strident racism of the Americans, as real too as the brightness and interest, the questioning and belief—above all the belief—of my audience at the Sorbonne, in the viability and the sanctity of the human spirit. Yes, the reality is all about us, timeless, ageless, waiting perhaps for that sensibility keen enough to proclaim it, to see people also as monuments destined for a future of nobility and dignity as impressive as that of the cathedrals of Chartres and Notre Dame.

Moving now, hurriedly! Away from the park, across the bridge separating the Right Bank from the Left; I tried to read the name newly acquired in my address book as I walked. It was a deep moonlit night in Paris; the streets were alive with revelry and song. I knew of a small cafe, just outside the bookstalls, close to the Seine. There one could hear the sloshing of the waves on a night such as this, could bask in the warmth generated by young lovers. And Paris is a city for lovers; for those who love life and for those who love each other. And on such a night none should be without a lover. I reached the telephone booth, began fantasizing. Only a short time from now, I dreamed, and we will be drinking wine in the cafe, laughing away the night, touching, slowly, cautiously; then into the night, face to face with the hazy whiteness, with the water, the noise; we will hold hands, perhaps, beneath the cathedral and glance, now and then, at the Eiffel Tower, seeing history before our eyes—and at some time, somewhere on this night, beneath this moon, there will be the closeness of two pairs of lips, the embrace, the telling mark of human mortality. "No, Askia," I had thought, listening anxiously to the ringing of the telephone, "I am not yet too old to dream."

May 15, 1974
I have said my good-bys to Raphael. We are no longer patient
and analyst. Perhaps, we will remain friends. I am doubtful. I feel
that I have used him. Unable for a while to trust the instinct for
survival that pulled me through the years, I sought him out—my
own private deus ex machina. But I came to him not so much to
be cured, but to be saved, for it was my life, not my mental state
that hung in the balance. He helped. However, in the final analysis, I had to save myself. That's what it boiled down to; what it always boils down to. Still, I am better for having known him. I feel
freer now. I sing in the shower again. I prepare to work non-stop
on the autobiography. I look admiringly at pretty girls again. I am
rested and refreshed from my trip to Paris. I am, I know, in
Raphael's debt.

June 2, 1974
Today is my birthday. I am forty-three years old. I leave for
Europe in a month. First Paris, then London. Paris to rest; London to work on the galleys of *The Way of the New World*. I am
writing steadily now. The autobiography is almost one-third
finished. Today, I watched my father die. I was back in the hospital, in that little room, wanting to move toward him, to touch
him. I remembered what Andrew Lavender had said: "You have
to come to grips with your father, one day." I think that I can do

that now; now that I have watched him die again, I think I can confront him and all that he meant to me.

June 5, 1974
Writing steadily. Movements between parts one and two are fuzzy. Must describe my experiences in Newark in more detail. How do I handle Momma? Can I use symbols for her? How do you portray the people you love as you once saw them, without hurting them? And how much of the truth can I tell—about myself, about Rosalie, about others? Well, I will put it all down. Then I will rewrite; and I will cut; and other parts can be published after I die. Morbid. Yes.

June 12, 1974
Took time out from the book. Stuck, must think. How much should I tell about the mulatto thing? It still bothers me. I thought that I had buried it in *The Way of the New World*. I haven't. I must work it out. But why here? Why not? It happened to me: the imaginings, fears, jealousies; I must work it out here.

June 13, 1974
Can't stay away from the book. Back to Phoebe now. Remembrances of things past. I wish I were a novelist. I could give a better accounting of what she meant to me. I'm not sure I have succeeded here. I have almost forgotten what she looks like. But I still remember what she meant to me. I still remember that!

June 15, 1974
Have hit a snag. Can't write. Should go out and get a drink. Should call up a girl. Working with my father again. He is dominating this book, too. It is not supposed to work out that way. Maybe I should tear up the whole thing and start again. But that would be silly. It *is* my life, and so I would just have to repeat everything, even the part concerning him. Damn!

June 18, 1974
Momma again! Symbols! Images! A house in Long Island. Marathon. White people all around, on the floor, in chairs. Weeping! Wailing! Men, women. Raphael is like a buddha/is a buddha. Sitting in the middle of the floor. A sad expression on his tanned

face. Thoughtful. People turn to look at me. I want to sink inside
myself. The voice comes from the outer limits, way beyond space,
beyond time, "Who has hurt you so much?" I look from face to
face. The weeping, wailing has stopped. Eyes, too from outer
space, focusing upon me, staring at me. Head bowed, eyes closed,
resignation, feebly, from inside, barely audible, "the madonna."
Cut this! *Yes. Cut this!*

June 19, 1974

Tore up four pages today. Am writing about her. More extensively
than before. Getting down to details. But should I? She is part of
my life's experiences; but she is white, and perhaps I should not
write about her. There is truth on one side and responsibility on
the other. Truth mandates that I tell all, put it all down. But responsibility means that I owe allegiance to those Black mothers
who see me as their son, those Black women who see me as their
lovers, those Black people who need images unpolluted by whites.
I am responsible to them, cannot give credence to the myth, give
validity to the old legends. Yet she happened. She was/is real. I
cannot deny that she lived within me. No, no apologies, no subtle
dealing with her; I will write of the experience; and healthy Black
people will understand that sometimes, not too often, but sometimes, men and women rise above the rainbow of color, and if
they are lucky, sometimes, though not too often, they find love.

June 22, 1975

Discussing the books. I am modest. I have difficulty discussing
books that I have written. Maybe I should simply note the criticism about them. No, that will not do. Must overcome my mod-
esty. Must rewrite this section; talk more about the books in
depth.

June 24, 1974

Going back over my diary. Damn! What terrible writing. Can I
leave it as it is? Some of it sounds pompous and silly. Maybe I
should change some of the words, make them more readable.
Must check with Loretta about this. Funny feeling, reading this.
Can't imagine that those things happened to me. I will leave the
diary to a Black college. Students will be titillated by some of it.

Scholars will be disappointed; not enough substance, they will say. How funny!

June 25, 1974
Picked up my tickets for London. Would like to leave right now, this minute. Feel ashamed, unclean, depressed. Up at five this morning; couldn't sleep. Headed for the typewriter. Couldn't get started. Section on Pat. Whole thing to include sections on Pat, Ruth, Rosalie. Maybe I should leave out the section on Pat. Feel ashamed. I wonder if she has the scars. What a monster I was. But I was frightened. Shit! That excuses nothing. I was brutal, sadistic. I am ashamed. I will let the section stay in. Maybe she will read it and understand . . . and maybe forgive . . .

June 28, 1974
About Ruth. Section almost completed. She deserved more from the world than she got. And she deserved better copy from me than she got. Damn, I wish this were a novel. I could write about all of these people in more detail. This way I am limited. Mostly I can only write about their impressions on me. And that is very distorted. I feel like Vivaldo. I am writing a book, but I have limited knowledge of the people I am writing about. I would like to have known a great deal about Ruth. I would like to have known her as a child; known the things she liked to do, the food she liked to eat, the kind of clothes she liked to wear, the people she liked and disliked. I would like to have known something about her early loves and hurts and disappointments. I wonder how she is and if she still has, after all these years, the quotation from Pasternak.

July 1, 1974
Next month this time, I will be in Paris. Working feverishly now. Want to finish part two before I go. No difficulty moving into section on Rosalie. Surprising. Thought I would have trouble. So far, not so bad. Back to the mulatto thing. It was a factor in her life too. Just like in Gwen Brooks' *Maude Martha*. And for all the Maude Marthas, even more devastating than for me. The strictures still remain for Black women, like Rosalie, whose skin is as dark as mine. And we have created this "race within a race" and none of the critics have the guts to condemn it.

July 3, 1974
Episode at Brooks Brothers. Don't think I conveyed what I
wanted to. Looking back now, I can hardly imagine all that I felt.
This is supposed to represent a turning point. Brooks Brothers—
the symbol of Anglo-Saxon success. Having achieved Brooks
Brothers, I had achieved American success. But that was all
delusion. I wish I could make that clear. Success for Black people
in this country is only tenuous; it is hollow and empty. But too
many of us will never believe that.

July 5, 1974
On *The Black Situation*. I still think it is my best book. Maybe
some of the essays are not as well written as they might have
been. Still, I think it was a good book. Took a break today. Gearing up for the section on the break with Rosalie. Will have to get
deep inside of myself. I'm anxious, but not afraid. Read-
ing/rereading part one. What a goddamn mess. Can I ever
straighten it out, organize it? It is so disorganized; I wish I could
begin rewriting now. And it is so depressing. There is little joy
here, and yet there was joy in my life. But that must come later. I
am trying to move too fast; I am too much in a hurry. I must go
through the breakup slowly, gradually, reliving it all, if I can,
again. But I don't want to. I would like to go to Paris now. I do
not want to write about this. I should call Raphael.

July 7, 1974
I wrote ten pages and tore them up!

July 12, 1974
I do not want to go through this again. I am not as healthy as I
thought I was. I should call Raphael. But what good would that
do? I would still have to write it and move on. I can't move on
until I write this section. But I can't write it either. There is too
much guilt! But is there such a thing as past guilt? I do not feel
guilty now. But I must write about the guilt of the past, and I
don't want to.

July 15, 1974
No change. For three days I have sat and looked into space, moving my hands over the typewriter, without touching the keys; the

paper is still blank. Today I didn't even try. Maybe I should call Les, have lunch. And if he is busy? I don't know. There aren't that many people to talk to! Maybe I should call Hoyt. But he must be pretty busy. I feel silly. I know that I can write this episode; but I don't want to. But why don't I want to? Could it be that writing to me means to finalize. That if I write it down, it will be over with, Rosalie and me, over with? And perhaps I do not want it to be over with. No . . .

July 16, 1974
Began the preliminaries leading to the breakup. I don't know how well I've done it. I can't reread it just yet. I will have to rewrite it, I know. It is as close to the truth as I can recall. I feel depressed.

July 17, 1974
Moving along pretty well, though a little shaky. Lots of extraneous material. Wish I really knew what Rosalie's reactions, thoughts were, during all of this. Can't try to guess. Only sure about my own. Difficult trying to stand back and observe them now. This is the saddest part of the book.

July 18, 1974
Finally! I covered the breakup. Part two almost complete. Now— the near mental breakup—mine. But if I deal with this I will put Raphael into the book. I would have to admit that I sought help from an analyst. But I don't want to admit this!

July 19, 1974
I have to think about the ending of part two again. I could close with my leaving the house. If I don't talk about the mental thing, it won't be dishonest. And if I do, then I must talk about therapy. But I don't want to talk about having gone to a therapist. Maybe I should just write about the breakup, and not mention Raphael. Yes.

July 21, 1974
I am exhausted. Have been working almost all day. Halfway through the episode leading to the breakdown. Part two is almost

finished. Leave for Paris in two weeks. Mentally tired and depressed. But part two is almost finished. Just about . . .

July 25, 1974

Finished part two yesterday. I am very tired, but the worst part is over. The rewriting will be easier now. Making preparations to leave for Paris. It's been a difficult three months.

While working on the material pertaining to my marriage, I had felt an overbearing compulsion to see Rosalie, to talk to her, to meet her face to face for the first time in two years. The desire became stronger once I finished my work, but doubts about my own motivations kept me, for a day or so, from making a decision. Had the writing brought back the old feelings of guilt? Did I feel strong enough, finally, to confront her without shame? Would seeing her again trigger the despair of yesterday? Would she be angry, insulting, accusing, and would a scene occur which would dampen my coming trip to Paris? Despite such doubts, I arranged to meet her, two days before my departure, in a small cafe on New York's East Side.

Nervous and apprehensive, I arrived early for the appointment. What did she look like now? As I pictured her in my mind? Did she have scars and were they as visible as mine once were? Did I dare stare directly into her eyes, challenge whatever I might find there? Two vodkas with a minimum amount of orange juice neither steadied my hands nor downed the nervousness. My eyes were fixed upon the entrance to the cafe, and I started each time a customer, Black or white, entered the door. Five minutes past the hour of five—our designated meeting time—she arrived. She strode boldly through the doors, paused, looked around, moved toward my beckoning finger. There was a smile on her face, a pronounced bravado in the way she carried herself. Unsteadily I arose, took her hand, kissed her on the cheek. "How are you?"

"I almost didn't find this place," she replied effusively, seating herself, directly across from me at the table. "So this is the kind of joint you hang out in these days?" We laughed together, both, perhaps, recalling one of my jokes of yesteryear: "A Black revolutionary like myself would not be caught dead in ritzy, high-class, bourgeois joints," I had once said. Her laughter came easy and because of it, my hands steadied, the panic subsided. She was a more handsome woman now than she had appeared before. There was a brightness in her eyes, a peaceful expression upon her face. The years may have wreaked havoc upon her, but such was no longer apparent. The scars which sometimes result from a marital dissolution had, for her, been wiped away by strength and determination. She was always, I reflected, more capable of surviving calamity than I was. Her ability to do so, and my inability to follow suit, was attributable to our varied perceptions of the world. Mine was the world of romanticism and dreams; hers was more practical and pragmatic. Her favorite writer was Ayn Rand. Mine was Richard Wright. The philosophy of her writer, simply put, taught that the world was to be manipulated, bested; that of mine adhered to the ideal that the world might/must be changed. Thus she, not I, understood the basics necessary for dealing with the Americans. I envied her, now, her philosopher, though I could not surrender mine.

Across the dinner of shad, set off by bottles of Bolla wine, the discussion ventured back to the past, came up to the present. We talked as though we had met last week, not two years ago. There was no bitterness or anguish in her voice. The jokes came readily, interspersed between more serious discussion about my writings, my lectures—my coming trip to Paris. The wine brought a warmth and relaxation, a peace, and I drifted off into thought, wondered, what it would be like to try again? Why not ask her, now, this moment, for a reconciliation? I could not. I did not believe that she would accept; but beyond that, I knew now that a future life together would differ little from that of the past. For what had happened between us had little to do with love or compatibility. I possessed a temperament forged out of the necessities of combating the world in which I lived; it was a temperament which demanded solitude, alienation, at times of my own choosing. It had led me, out of fear, to become a writer.

Yes, Raphael was right. The need to protect myself had driven me away from those I loved and into a preoccupation (writing) which was, as Baldwin once defined it, an act of terror. But it was an unnatural act as well. The writer sat, isolated, for long periods of time, back bent over, feet planted squarely upon the floor, arms hunched forward—like some giant orangutan—eyes cemented upon reams and reams of white paper. His mind must remain fixated for hours upon a single thought, a single event, a single character, sometimes a single word. And if one were a Black writer, there were other factors to be considered. For him, the act of writing was also a way of combating the terror of the world outside. It was a way of denying the society its ultimate victory— the destruction of one's humanity—by leaving, as Haki Madhu- buti has written, a record of man's transgression against the human spirit. But more, it was proof of the Black will to resist, to remain beyond the barricade with the oppressed and dispossessed, to be the one solitary voice, shouting to the storm troopers and the lynch mob, in affirmation of the dignity and decency of man- kind.

Rosalie was talking, now, gesticulating, but I heard little of what she said. I was thinking about what might have been, had we been away from the Americans, been allowed to grow up healthy and free, had not had to live our daily lives in preparation for combat. There might have been, despite the exigencies of writ- ing, a future for us together. Neither the terror of writing nor the terror of living in America had managed to destroy our love, for love remained, despite all that had gone before. And though this love was not strong enough to keep us together, it was strong enough to sustain me in the most frightening of moments.

I took her hand, brought it to my lips. I knew now that the road once traveled could not be journeyed again. For me, there would be no more Rosalies; I would remain alone, warring with shadows—confronting the terror of living, alone. Yet I was nei- ther sad nor despondent. I felt a sense of relief, even of exhila- ration. I was resigned to the fact, at last, that terror was a con- stant in human life, and that each person must deal with it as best he could. My way was not that of Ayn Rand, but of Richard Wright, and there was consolation in being able to accept this fact. When I left Rosalie at the subway station, later that eve- ning, en route back to her home/our home in Harlem, I knew nothing had really ended two years ago. The form of our rela- tionship, but not the substance had changed. I loved her still, very much. But I had places to go and things to do. And I need to travel to those places and do those things—alone.

I arrived in Paris for the third time in two years, en route to London, some days before the fall of Richard Nixon. My Paris friends had deserted the city, some going to Dijon, others to the Riviera and Spain, joining the late summer exodus which usually leaves the city to those who cannot afford to leave it and to the tourists. I remember feeling almost exuberant after my meeting with Rosalie, not so melancholy as I had the year before, more restful. I was more inclined to make eyes at the beautiful girls, rather than passes. I spent a great deal of time in the parks, in the sidewalk cafes, moving in and out of the crowds on St. Michel, walking along the banks of the Seine. But I spent a great deal of time, also, in my hotel room, situated far out on the Left Bank, near the Eiffel Tower, where my window looked down upon the courtyard of a convent.

The convent was set in an oasis of green and surrounded by trees and flowers. It was insulated, so it seemed, from the noise of the city, isolated from the stone and steel outside its walls. Here, each evening, an ancient ritual was enacted: Long before there were bodies to which voices belonged, somber chords of what seemed like some medieval song, sounded from behind the rich green foliage, the high, thick, dark green shrubbery and gnarled, but stately oak trees. Gradually the bodies and voices became one and nuns, dressed in black gowns, preceded by a much older woman, whose black gown was touched off by a spotless white hat and collar, walked in single file, the column broken only in two places: one in which two young nuns held a platform bearing the figurine of the Virgin, and some distance down the line, where another platform bore a figurine of a saint. On some evenings the procession was joined by older men and women in civilian clothes, whose cracked voices stood out in stark contrast to the high, shrill voices of the nuns.

Around and around the gardens of freshly appearing greens, yellows, and reds they moved, as if they were the pallbearers of the centuries, with grace and dignity, never breaking the cadence of their march, never faltering in the gusto with which they sang. I felt as if I were witness to history past, as if I had become a voyeur, intruding upon some secret ritual of the church, unknown these many years. I thought of my mother and her still unshaken faith in her God and I wondered if she were conscious of the tradition of beauty and splendor that belief in and worship of that God had inspired. I knew that if she were here now, she would have felt, while gazing upon this ceremony, a certain vindication of her faith, would have found distinct meaning in this ritual which occurred nightly, during this period when the Watergate episode rushed to its swift denouement. She would have interpreted the events below not so much as a ritual, but as a wake, as God's way of signaling the faithful. The sinful would, indeed, be punished, the grievances of the just, redressed, and still, as in the days of old, that Lord God Jehovah was he to whom the act of vengeance belonged.

For millions of Black people—my mother included—the fall of Richard Nixon was vindication of the ancient scripture, validation of the existence of God. Though she had been an apolitical person for most of her life, Richard Nixon the politician had transformed her, overnight, into a politician watcher. More from instinct than from logic or reason, she had declared that, in her words, "He don't mean us no good," and had understood, though she could not have articulated it, that he was the creation of white people, much more a Native Son than Bigger Thomas could have ever been. She voted for the first time in her life, against Richard Nixon in the campaign that sent John Kennedy to the White House, again in 1960, and once again in 1972, believing each time that she had registered a protest against immorality and injustice. And she had talked to me, via long-distance telephone, in that self-righteous way of hers, during each stage of the Watergate revelations, reminding me of her righteous prophecy, of the instinct which led her, long before most Americans, to the conclusion that Richard Nixon was an evil man and that one day, the God of all men would render him his just deserts.

And now, as the Paris papers daily chronicle the last chapters in the political life of Richard Nixon, as American guests in the hotel whisper despairingly of the calamities to come, as the Black expatriates in Leroy Haynes Soul Food Restaurant near Place Pigalle drink toasts to the coming apocalypse, I sit at my window, overlooking the courtyard. I am witness to history past and to history unfolding. The history of the demise of Richard Nixon, however, will not move me, as does this ancient ritual of the church, for I bear no grudge against Nixon. Unlike my mother, I have never viewed him as evil, but instead as the representative of a people arrogant enough to believe that the ritual they are about to perform, the ceremonial act of bloodletting, will absolve them of their ancient sins, will convince the world that their democracy works.

The symbolism of the ceremony I watch from my window will

be duplicated in that soon to take place in America. Only the form and the meaning will be different. As in the ritual below, there will be long columns, composed of both Blacks and whites; there will be clichés clothed in pious, sonorous tones: "Our system works." "We are a nation of law and justice." Instead of figurines of the saints and the Virgin, hoisted upon platforms, as in the pageant below, there will be drawings in America, showing the statue of the blind lady of justice, and some distance away, the prostrate figure of Richard Nixon. He will be transformed into an anti-hero, one whose transgression has allowed a country to exonerate itself. Is he creative enough to know that this is his finest hour? Does he have imagination enough to understand that by becoming the sacrificial lamb for his countrymen, he allows them to whitewash the past, by declaiming piously that "we have a system which works, a nation where God still reigns, where the transgressor, be he pauper or President, is dealt with equally, where no man is above the law?"

The ruse, however, will not work. There are those more sophisticated than my mother. They will not see in the fall of Nixon, the working out of God's vengeance, but, instead, the result of human arrogance. They will know that no divine intervention has occurred, that there will be no redemption, that America will not be cleansed and purified. For Richard Nixon was not simply an individual; no, he was a metaphor. He is what America is: a land of the expedient, form and no substance, a huckster's paradise. There, pretension and appearance constitute norms of behavior and, historically, people have shirked responsibilities for their own sins by selecting scapegoats—whether such scapegoats be Blacks or Presidents.

Nixon is America incarnate, and his demise will not remove the strain from the history of that nation which produced him. No number of Watergates can erase the blotches from its whitened facade; no number of dethronements can compensate for its bloody past. There are not enough jails to hold the countless Watergate conspirators in and out of government who daily play their dirty tricks upon the millions of poor and destitute throughout the world, with the acquiescence of the American public. No, no one man has impugned America's history, besmirched its Constitution. The most endearing clauses in that Constitution have, historically, allowed Americans to fool themselves, to believe that their history was different from what it was. And such clauses,

concerning justice, equality, and freedom, have led them to believe that that man who attempted to sabotage the opposition
party was a more sinful man, a more evil man, than such
slaveholders as Thomas Jefferson and George Washington.

Such reasoning defies logic; yet logic and the Americans have
never been compatible bedfellows. The huckster is the anti-
logician who, through manipulation of words, actions, and events,
displays contempt for things of the mind. They are legion in
America. They appear at each calamitous event, rationale in hand.
They are politicians and college professors, artists and writers.
They made their initial appearance during the time of slavery and
produced sermons, songs, books, and scholarly treatises designed
to prove that America was an innocent nation, conceived in morality, despite the act of enslaving and murdering hundreds of
thousands of people. During the Civil War, the hucksters
glorified the architects of genocide—the Ku Klux Klan, the
Knights of the White Camellia. They offered their rationales also
during the great world wars, when Black men who escaped dying
for democracy abroad were murdered in the name of democracy
on American shores. They were capable of rationalizing the beating of children by mobs, the sheriffs who unleased dogs upon
human beings, asking in such journals as *Commentary* and *Saturday Review* if Black people were not, indeed, inferior, and thus
historically deserving of the treatment they received.

They are prepared now to explain Richard Nixon, to attempt to
exonerate themselves before the world. They will forget the rationale which they helped to disseminate and which the country
accepted, concerning Nixon before the fall: he was the great
white hope, the deus ex machina, who would put the niggers back
in their place, bring an end to Black ambition and Black militancy. They would forget too that he tried, and achieved some
success in such endeavors, and that in so doing he returned
America to the traditions of old—those enunciated in the Constitution and drawn up by slavemasters.

By the time I landed at Heathrow Airport in London on August 15, Richard Nixon had been dethroned for almost a week.
London papers continued to carry headlines of the affair, feature
stories, essays, quotes about the private anguish of the one-time
President, now in exile in San Clemente. Americans whom I met
in the hotel were eager to discuss Watergate and its aftermath,
but the English seemed not overly concerned despite the head-

lines in newspapers, much more concerned, in fact, about the spiraling cost of foods and necessities brought on by a worldwide
inflation.

I would come to know the English and their city only
superficially on this short visit. In the hotels, in the pubs throughout the Soho district, in the shops and restaurants, on the streets,
they maintained a quiet dignity, a politeness bordering on condescension.

Still, there was a calmness here, an absence of hustle and hurry
that I found infecting. I worked daily on the galleys of my book
The Way of the New World, which arrived from America days
before I arrived from Paris, and in the evening, I strolled around
the Soho district, through Hyde Park. A few days after my arrival,
while traveling through the Soho district, on successive days, I
met first Miranda and later Pauline. Miranda worked in the district. She was a product of an Oxford education, and was involved
in distributing American films for a London audience. Pauline
worked as supervisor for a London clearing house. I became close
friends with both of them, anxious to escape, if only momentarily,
the drudgery of rereading material I had written over two years
ago. In the daytime I would travel down to Flaxen Street, to the
little pub nearby, to have lunch with Miranda. We strolled often,
arm in arm, down the ramparts of Trafalgar Square, dining on
French, Indian, and Chinese cuisine, talked of books and writers,
theater and rock music, America and London, Algeria and Spain.
At night, often, Pauline and I would go down by the Thames, sit,
looking out into the quiet water, to a theater, to Little Venice,
talking of Africa and the Third World, arguing about the rele-
vance of Frantz Fanon, and contrasting the Black situation in
England and America. Together, Pauline and Miranda helped to
make my stay in London among the most enjoyable experiences
of my life.

And joy was a constant now, despite the knowledge that in less
than three weeks, I would be back in America, working on the autobiography, reliving the most frightening, terrifying moments of
my life. I would be forced to resume the confrontation with my
feelings toward Rosalie, my parents, the many people who had
moved in and out of my life in these forty-two years. And yet I
looked upon the coming days with calm, little anxiety, free of despair, of melancholia. After all, in the best of the poetic tradition,
I had looked into myself, confronted the demons hidden there,

wandered around in the quagmire of my own mind, and emerged more whole. Why should I not then be relatively happy, satisfied with myself, not for short periods, but for long stretches of time? I concluded that I was, and that this time, unlike the times years back, the happiness and the satisfaction were not simple manic manifestations, interludes between joy and despair. Such feelings —well-being, happiness—were accelerated when, after a week, I completed proofreading the galleys of my book, turned them over to my London editor, realized that they would shortly be on the way to New York, and that in three months' time, I would have published my seventh book. I recalled passages from a statement by Richard Wright, lines of which I had repeated so often in the past, "I am filled with the joy of living," held them close to my consciousness, my bosom, repeated them silently as I strolled the London streets alone, in the absence of either Miranda or Pauline. I was thinking about these words still, on that day when I wandered over to sit on the spiral in Piccadilly Circus, joining the youngsters who sat there, it seems, always night and day, unmoved by the pigeons who wandered about pecking at unseeable crumbs beneath their feet.

The words were in my mind, too, when the young people beckoned me to the top of the pyramid, as I moved up the steps, grasping the hands of a pretty girl. I sat and looked at the passersby, the spectators who stopped, as always, to gaze at this tourist attraction. Impulsively, the young people raised their voices in song and I, not knowing the words, began, nevertheless, slowly to hum the tune. Soon I had learned at least the refrain of the song, and with Wright's words still ringing in my consciousness, I threw embarrassment aside, joined as one with the singers, shouted out to the multitude of spectators. I was surprised, bewildered, even, when some of the spectators responded, arms waving, voices loud, and helped to transform Piccadilly Circus into an arena of song, of laughter, of joy. And I stood there, thinking of Richard Wright, of his words, and carried aloft by the setting, the exhilaration of the moment, shouted from deep somewhere down the yesterdays and the yesteryears, my voice thundering into my ears, lost in the medley, the cacophony of sound, yet vivid, poignant, silent, but aloud, in my heart, my mind, "I want to live! Yes!"

New York, 1976.

S